# Amazing Rituals *Of* INDIA

Swayam Ganguly was born and raised in Jamshedpur and currently lives in Kolkata. He wears many hats: a published author, director of corporate films, editorial consultant for various publishers, an aficionado of sports and an enthusiast of Indian culture.

The spontaneous induction of the Gayatri mantra at a young age made him curious and passionate about the diverse culture and rituals of India. However, his dispassionate research backed by a rational mind allows him no fanatical glorification or preaching.

# Amazing Rituals *of* INDIA

Swayam Ganguly

hachette INDIA

First published in India in 2025 by Hachette India
(Registered name: Hachette Book Publishing India Pvt. Ltd)
An Hachette UK company
www.hachetteindia.com

1



All chapters have been researched and written by Swayam Ganguly.



ISBN: 978-93-5731-924-9

Hachette Book Publishing India Pvt. Ltd
4th & 5th Floors, Corporate Centre,
Plot No. 94, Sector 44, Gurgaon - 122003, India

Typeset in ITC Galliard Std 11.2/15
by InoSoft Systems, Noida

Printed and bound in India
by Thomson Press India Ltd.

FSC
www.fsc.org
MIX
Paper | Supporting responsible forestry
FSC® C010615

Dedicated to my mother, Namita Ganguly, who taught me the basic rituals of life.

# CONTENTS

## 4. RELIGIOUS RITUALS 103

## 5. FOOD AND DRINK RITUALS 129



## 6. SOCIAL RITUALS 136

# IMAGE COPYRIGHT INFORMATION

Chapter title design: Saylee Rampurikar/Shutterstock.com

Special information box design: LiukaArt/Shutterstock.com

Heading underline: bogadeva1983/Shutterstock.com

Small information box design: Olena Vyshynska/Shutterstock.com

Page 4: A festival of the Nyishi tribe of Arunachal Pradesh: Prashanthns/Wikimedia (https://en.wikipedia.org/wiki/Nyishi_people)

Page 13: Manipuri wedding: snapgalleria/Shutterstock.com

Page 14: Manipuri marriage procession: Sachin Pics/Shutterstock.com

Page 15: Manipuri wedding items: kissor meetei/Shutterstock.com

Page 19: Gae holud: ABIR ROY BARMAN/Shutterstock

Page 23: Dhaniram Toto: Rajibnandi/CCA-SA 3.0 Unreported licence (https://commons.wikimedia.org/wiki/File:A_Toto_man.jpg)

Page 29: Bhagoria: Ajaychouhan811/CCA-Share Alike 4.0 International (https://en.wikipedia.org/wiki/Bhagoria_Festival)

Page 41: Finding the ring: Svetype26/Shutterstock

Page 42: Christian wedding: antographer/Shutterstock.com

Page 43: Haldi: stockpexel/Shutterstock.com

Page 43: Pheras: SyedAliAshraf/Shutterstock.com

Page 44: Kanyadan: vijay makwana/Shutterstock.com

Page 44: Sindoordan Purushottam Malav/Shutterstock.com

Page 45: Mehndi: Duan Wade/Shutterstock.com

Page 45: Nikah: FAROG HASAN/Shutterstock.com

Page 46: Currency note garland: photography hd/Shutterstock.com

Page 53: Lai Haraoba: Ramesh Lalwani/CCA 2.0 Generic (https://en.wikipedia.org/wiki/Lai_Haraoba)

Page 61: Manipuri raas leela: CC-BY/CCA 2.0 Generic Licence (https://en.wikipedia.org/wiki/Manipuri_dance#/media/File:Rasa_Lila_in_Manipuri_dance_style.jpg)

Page 63: Cheraw: Tlinga/CCA-SA 3.0 Unreported licence (https://commons.wikimedia.org/wiki/File:Cheraw_jampui.jpg)

Page 64: Mithun horns: explorewithinfo/Shutterstock.com

Page 66: Garba: Sumit Saraswat/Shutterstock.com

Page 67: Dandiya: India Picture/Shutterstock.com

Page 70: Siddis: Vickey Chauhan/Shutterstock.com

Page 72: Kokna festival: ACShinde/CCA-SA 4.0 International licence (https://en.wikipedia.org/wiki/Kokna_(tribe)#/media/File:Moment_from_Kokna_festival.jpg)

Page 76: Odissi: ShaikhMeraj/Shutterstock.com

Page 84: Dinga Gavar: Vipingoyal/CCA-SA 3.0 Unreported licence (https://en.wikipedia.org/wiki/Dhinga_Gavar#/media/File:Dhinga_Gavar.JPG)

Page 85: Dahi Handi: AKS.9955/SSA-SA 4.0 International licence (https://en.wikipedia.org/wiki/Dahi_Handi#/media/File:Dahi_Handi.JPG)

Page 94: Dhunuchi naach: India Picture/Shutterstock

Page 98: Maha Kumbh: Yosarian/CCA-SA 3.0 Unreported licence (https://en.wikipedia.org/wiki/Kumbh_Mela#/media/File:Kumbh_Mela2001.JPG)

Page 110: Puri rath yatra: G.-U. Tolkiehn/GFDL and Creative Commons (CCA-SA 3.0 Unreported licence) (https://en.wikipedia.org/wiki/Ratha_Yatra#/media/File:Rath_Yatra_Puri_07-11027.jpg)

Page 112: Hemis festival: Sandeep-Bisht/Shutterstock.com

Page 113: Muharram: Jayakumar/Shutterstock

Page 122: Korku women dancing: Ramesh Lalwani/CCA-SA 2.0 Generic licence (https://commons.wikimedia.org/wiki/File:Korku_Dance_Madya_pradesh.jpg)

Page 127: Bonda woman: Yves Picq http://veton.picq.fr/GNU Free Documentation License (https://en.wikipedia.org/wiki/Bonda_people#/media/File:Inde_bondo_8859a.jpg)

Page 128: Bonda haat: https://www.shutterstock.com/image-photo/bonda-tribes-womens-haat-market-atonkudelli-1752150782

Page 142: Munda family: Bradley-Birt, Francis Bradley/PD (https://en.wikipedia.org/wiki/Munda_people#/media/File:Group_Photo_of_Mundas_-_Chota_Nagpur_1903.jpg)

Page 148: Bishnoi women: OmMishra/Shutterstock

Page 150: Kokna people: Ramesh Lalwani/CCA 2.0 Generic Licence (https://en.wikipedia.org/wiki/Kokna_(tribe)#/media/File:Kokna_Tribals_from_Nandurbar_Maharashtra-1.jpg)

Page 154: Santhal folk dance: Manishankar Patra/Shutterstock.com

Page 156: Santhal masks: Rudra Narayan Mitra/Shutterstock.com

Page 157: Santhal hut: Manishankar Patra/Shutterstock.com

Page 157: Konayak headhunters: ABHISHEK BASAK 90/Shutterstock.com

Page 171: Page: Bison-horn Maria: Hari Mahidhar/Shutterstock.com

Page 173: Lepcha kid: Kittu's/Shutterstock.com

Page 180: Konyak chief with black teeth: Yves Picq/CCA-SA 3.0 Unreported 2.5 generic 2.0 Generic and 1.0 Generic licence (https://commons.wikimedia.org/wiki/File:Koniak_0382b.jpg)

Page 184: Lath Mar Holi: Narender9/CCA-SA 3.0 Unported licence (https://commons.wikimedia.org/wiki/File:Latmar_women_in_action_in_Barsana.jpg)

Page 191: Charak: Saikat Paul/Shutterstock.com

Page 196: Jallikattu: ELAMARAN ELAA PHOTOGRAPHY/Shutterstock.com

# PREFACE

This unique compilation of amazing rituals covering the length and breadth of the country is thematically aligned yet varied. While some rituals are light, some may seem dark, gritty and, to some, regressive; equally there are many that are elaborate, sophisticated and nuanced.

The book does not claim to cover the complete list of rituals, but its focus is to spotlight the most striking or surprising and introduce some among the lesser-known ones. Thus, while mainstream rituals have not been skipped altogether, they are relatively fewer. Also included are some rituals that may no longer be in practice but reveal some unmissable aspects of India's past.

This book does not attempt to judge any culture or ritual. The inclusion of any facts does not intend to show them as being more important than others that may have been excluded. While there are thousands of rituals that are integral to India, this selection tries to cover as many peoples and regions as possible while also maintaining the amazing factor, which is subjective.

The book intends being respectful towards all communities and tribes of India, and any depiction or description of any ritual or part of daily life, any belief or occupation, any food or fashion is never meant to be demeaning. The occasional use of wit and humour in the narrative is solely to enhance the reading experience.

The classification spread of rituals into nine sections do have many areas of inevitable overlap. The categorization was decided on the basis of which aspect of the ritual the reader would relate to, or be interested in, the most. A dance ritual in a socio-religious festival thus may be categorized both as a religious performance and as part of a music and dance tradition. The same can also be seen as a social or cultural event.

The writer has tried to be as accurate as possible. However, if any information seems incorrect to a reader in the know, we would highly appreciate if they could bring that to our notice. We will correct the information in the next edition.

And now, we invite you to enjoy this eye-opening phantasmagoria that both educates and entertains!

# 1

# MARRIAGE RITUALS

> I am He, you are She, I am Song, you are Verse, I am Heaven, you are Earth. We two shall here together dwell, becoming parents of children.
>
> – ***Atharva Veda XIV 2, 71***

## AMAZING NYISHI WEDDING RITUALS

In India's predominantly patriarchal culture, the Nyishis of Arunachal Pradesh stand out for their belief in granting equal rights and status to the women of the clan. The Nyishis believe that women are symbols of strength, prosperity and peace. The men of the family take suggestions from their female counterparts before arriving at any decision regarding the family, be it small or big.

Marriage is considered a sacred bond by the Nyishis. And child marriage is still not too uncommon.

A Nyishi wedding begins with a boiled egg examination, chicken liver examination and pig liver examination. These three tests are performed to predict if the marital alliance will be favourable.

First, the groom's family pays the bride's home a visit with *hopha*, which is a token of respect consisting of sugar and a flower platter called *baan moya*. The *miri*, or the marriage negotiator, helps both the families to decide on compensation for the bride. Though dowry is banned in India, traces of such practices remain. This exchange of money is believed to ensure that the bride is happy in her new home. It takes another meeting to fix the marriage date, followed by the exchange of gifts, such as clothes, an assortment of meats, swords, ornaments and animals. In earlier times, the list of gifts also included the bride's family sending a slave to the groom's family. The abolition of slavery has put an end to this ritual.

Nyishi weddings are called *Nyeda* and are typically performed at the bride's house.

Later, when the bride arrives at the groom's place, the *changtun phahi*, or purification ritual, is performed. The bride is

> The Nyishis believe that nature is composed of both humans and spirits, and it's essential to maintain a perfect state of coexistence with nature. They also believe in life after death and worship spirits. The Nyishis sacrifice animals to appease these supernatural spirits and deities.

asked to sacrifice an animal as the priest chants a prayer.

The *changtum bheenam*, or the thanksgiving ceremony, is the last part of the wedding ceremony, where gifts and ornaments are exchanged as a token of gratitude. Then begins the grand feast! The Nyishis dress sharply at weddings, symbolizing their connection to their ancestral roots.

### The Nyishi Tribe: An Introduction

The Nyishis are a unique tribe of Arunachal Pradesh. They are also known as Dafla and Bangni. They speak Tibeto-Burman and support their livelihood mainly by farming and hunting. They practise a slash-and-burn form of agriculture, while some are hunters and fishermen. The Nyishis like living in hilly regions and can usually be found at an elevation of 3,000–6,000 feet above sea level. They live in houses built of pilings and worship the spirits of nature. The tribe follows a clan-based system of relationships. There are three major clans – Dollu, Dopum and Dodum.

### How Well Do You Know the North-East?

The north-eastern region (NER) comprises the seven sister states of Assam, Arunachal Pradesh, Manipur, Nagaland, Meghalaya, Mizoram and Tripura. Sikkim is also part of the NER, because the state has similar tribes, but not part of the seven sisters. Various tribes make up almost

A festival of the Nyishi tribe of Arunachal Pradesh

50 per cent of the total population of this region. The four states of Arunachal Pradesh, Nagaland, Mizoram and Meghalaya have a tribal population of more than 80 per cent. A common characteristic of tribes in this region is that they have Mongoloid origins and features. The high-altitude terrains some of these tribes reside in have made them adapt to the conditions and choose particular professions to survive, such as hunting, gathering and settled cultivation, along with secondary occupations, such as animal husbandry and terrace cultivation. The tribes of Arunachal Pradesh include the Monpas, Nishyis, Padams, Sherdukpens and Miniyongs. The Mizos engage in shifting cultivation in Mizoram, as do the Nagas in Nagaland, the Jamatias in Tripura and the Kukis in Manipur. Several tribes in Meghalaya, such as the Khasis and the Garos, also practise shifting cultivation. In places of higher altitudes,

especially in states like Arunachal Pradesh and Sikkim, the tribes practise cattle rearing as agriculture is largely restricted because of the terrain. The Lepchas and Bhutias of Sikkim practise horticulture under terrace cultivation. The tribal communities of the NER like drinking home-made beverages prepared with rice, maize or millet as ingredients. Some tribes in Arunachal Pradesh and Sikkim drink salted butter tea. The common vegetables consumed are varieties of roots, tubers, bamboo shoots and mushrooms. Furthermore, they consume dried fish, beef and pork. The tribes often cover their bodies with animal skin to ward off the cold in the high altitudes. They wear long robes, hats or headgear made of animal skin and locally made footwear. The houses in the rural areas are conically shaped and constructed on a base of wooden logs with stone, while wooden planks make up the floors.

## MARRIAGE RITUALS OF THE KHASIS

There are many customs, rituals and traditions followed by the Khasi tribe of Assam. According to one of their traditions, every child in the tribe is recognized by the mother's name and not the father's, when the latter is more common in India. The Khasi mother inherits the child and the family property, not the father – again a shift from what has traditionally been a common practice in India. The law of this tribe states that marriages are a completely civil contract. Men usually marry between the ages of eighteen and thirty-five, and women between thirteen and eighteen. Though arranged marriages are a trend among the Khasis, young people also have the liberty to choose their life partners. The tribe was once a patriarchal society, and it is intriguing how this patriarchy dissolved over time. As more and more men lost their lives to wars and battles, they left behind widows who were forced to remarry. But there were social repercussions as the children who had lost their fathers were strangely labelled 'illegitimate' after their mothers remarried. Hence, the Khasi people decided not to tolerate such discrimination and declared that henceforth children should take up their mother's last name. The wars and battles have long ended, and the life expectancy of the Khasi male has gone up. But this ritual still stands the test of time.

### The Khasi Tribe: An Overview

The Khasis of Assam are among the earliest immigrants who settled in East Assam from the neighbouring country of Myanmar. After settling down in most parts of the state, they established their own kingdom until British rule. Meghalaya too has a large population of the Khasi people.

## MARRIAGE RITUALS OF THE DIMASA

The Dimasa tribe of Assam has a total of forty male clans, together called *sengphong*. Forty-two female clans together are called *julu*, *jilik* or *jadi*. One cannot marry within the same clan, from either the father's side or the mother's. A girl is normally married when she is between fifteen and twenty years of age. Urban areas have witnessed a change with the age factor extending up to thirty years, especially among educated women.

The consent of the boy and the girl is taken into account. The decision, even if it is a rejection of the proposal for whatever reason, is communicated with utmost honesty.

> The practice of marrying outside one's own community, clan or tribe is called exogamy.

After the marriage proposal is sealed, the groom's side sends a packet of salt wrapped in plantain leaves joined by seven threads to the bride's family. This is called *sandibasemba* or *semjudigarba*. If the bride's side accepts it, a few days later the groom's side brings home-made rice beer, or *judi*, to the bride's home – meant for the elder members of her side. The drink, on this occasion, is called *laothaoi*, and the ritual is called *laothai langba*. This is when they often decide the date of the marriage. Earlier the date was decided at another ritual called *laothai langagini*, which is not common anymore.

### Assam

Assam is a multi-linguistic and multi-ethnic state boasting of over thirty tribal groups. The Bodos are the dominant Assamese people, followed by the Mishings or Miris. Then there are the Karbis or Mikir, Rabhas, Kacharis, Garos, Khasis and Dimasas.

## KALTI: THE 'BRIDE PRICE' OF THE DIMASA

After the marriage is agreed upon, every Dimasa girl must be given *kalti*, or the bride price, in the form of rupees. However, rupees here mean coins, not paper notes. This is the traditional custom of the Dimasas. If *kalti* is not given by the groom's party or not accepted by the bride's party, it means not being included in the forty male clans or forty-two female clans. Therefore, the acceptance of *kalti* is a right for a Dimasa woman. The *kalti* is not fixed, and the amount is agreed upon after negotiations between both parties.

The marriage ceremony takes place in the bride's house. On the eve of the wedding, a party of elderly people from the bridegroom's side visits the bride's house to enquire if everything is all right within the family. This custom is called *gilimgasanaiba*. If any family member or relative of the bride falls ill, the ceremony is postponed. Otherwise, the bridegroom's party sets off for the bride's house the next day.

The bridegroom's party includes his family members, close relatives and village elders. The bridegroom is escorted to the bride's house dressed in new clothes. The marriage ceremony is almost like a village festival. Men and women are decked up in their best clothes and ornaments. In the courtyard of the bride's house, the older family members from both sides are seated according to their seniority. The seating arrangement displays the closeness of the elderly people to the bridegroom or the bride. The guests of the bridegroom are seated to the right, while the bride's guests sit to the left. Then the bridegroom is carried to the courtyard by four strong boys. The groom bows down before his parents, his would-be parents-in-law and his elder relatives in turn – according to how close he is to each person. Two boys flanking the groom place a bamboo mat for the bridegroom to kneel before the elders. Two other boys hold up a cloth called *rimsao* to prevent others from seeing the feet when this ritual is done.

The old people bless the bridegroom. They often recite long-verse sermons. After the blessings, the bridegroom sits on the special mat brought for him. His parents and parents-in-law sit beside him. The village headman then advises the groom often on things he should do as a model husband and things he shouldn't do after marriage. The bride, decked up in her wedding dress and ornaments, is brought before the groom. The ritual of *yaopaba*, or giving away the bride, takes place as the bride's parents chant a beautiful verse to request the parents of the bridegroom to welcome their daughter to her new household.

On the day of the wedding, the Dimasa god Brai-Sibrai is worshipped to bless the bride and the bridegroom, and this worship is known as *mayaofagarba*. The *hojai*, or priest, performs this ritual by sacrificing a duck or cock in the courtyard of the bride's house to pray to the deities and keep the evil spirits away. That sacrificial duck or cock and *judi* becomes the main part of the menu of the wedding feast. It is interesting to note that judi is almost a constant in all Dimasa ceremonies. Before the guests dig into the ceremonial feast, the couple separately worships the god *Mido*. The sacrificial meat of pigs is often a part of the ritual. *Judi* and meat are offered to God Sibrai.

The guests then have a hearty meal of fish, meat and *judi*, courtesy the bride's family. After they have eaten to their heart's content, the bridegroom's party returns home, leaving the bridegroom at the bride's house. Cohabitation is not permitted on the wedding day. The bridegroom stays at the bride's home for three nights and then returns home with the bride. This custom is called *firathangba*. This is followed by a custom called *minhabra*, wherein the couple traditionally stayed at the bride's house for a year. This is not very common anymore. These days, the couple spend just two to three days at the bride's house as a token gesture towards the traditional custom and then move out.

In Dimasa society, women of different matriclans (mother's or female clan – *julu*) do not live in the same house, neither do they use common clothes, ornaments and cosmetics. Since they can't marry within the same matri- or patriclan, a married woman naturally lives separately with her husband, in a newly built house either near her parents' house or near her in-laws' house. There is no joint family system nor dowry among the Dimasas. However, the mother of the bride gives her clothes and other essential household items normally used by women when they reside in a separate home.

Hence, a Dimasa family is a neolocal type of family. Polygamy is rare. However, if either of the spouses dies early, then the other can remarry. One can also remarry the widow of the deceased elder brother (levirate) but not that of a younger male sibling. Similarly, a man can marry the younger sister of his deceased wife (sororate) but not the elder one. Divorce is possible but rare. Divorce can be obtained when the aggrieved man or woman makes an appeal to the *khunang*, the village headman, who discusses the matter with the village elders and tries to work out a compromise between the couple. If the compromise fails, divorce is granted. The guilty party has to pay a sum of money as a fine. The divorcee can remarry in compliance with social customs. If divorce is granted, the custody of the male child and the female child are given to the father and the mother respectively.

Though the Dimasa society permits marriage between a boy and a girl belonging to different patriclans and matriclans only, a social convention called *hain daopri* allows cross-cousin marriages. This is possible when the *sengphong* of the boy is different from the girl or the *julu* of the boy is also not the same *julu* as that of the girl. This is rare, not to mention confusing.

The Dimasas follow the rules of clan exogamy perhaps too rigidly, and violating these rules leads to excommunication from the tribe. The Dimasas also do not allow anyone in the tribe to marry a non-Dimasa.

> Marriage by 'capture' is also rare but occurs. However, in both cases, the marriage has to be formalized according to the Dimasa rules. Failure to do so will lead to the couple not having a place in Dimasa society.

If such an event occurs, they have no place in Dimasa society. But there is light at the end of the tunnel. Thanks to a custom called *tharba*, a new *julu* is created for a non-Dimasa girl if a Dimasa boy marries her, and this includes her in Dimasa society. But such marriages are rather rare. There is no such custom for a non-Dimasa boy.

## DESCENDANTS OF THE PANDAVAS?

The Toda tribe is considered the most ancient Indian tribe. This tribe resides in the Nilgiri Hills of Tamil Nadu. It has its own language and secretive rules, regulations and customs. In the olden days, the Todas believed themselves to be the descendants of the Pandavas from the Mahabharata, who had Draupadi as their common wife. Due to this belief that they were the descendants of the Pandavas, the Todas had a tradition where one woman had to marry all the males in a family, and they all became her husband.

## MARRIAGE IN MANIPUR

The Manipuris prefer to marry within their own community, but they are also not against inter-caste marriages. Normally, the first step in the wedding process is the meeting of the prospective bride and groom. The grand event where these young men or women get a chance to meet their prospective life partners is the Manipuri New Year Festival.

### Wedding Attire

A Manipuri bride wears a bright and colourful wedding dress with a skirt called *raslila* on her wedding day and a red and black sarong called *pindhan*, matched with a blouse called *silum*. The groom usually dresses in a dhoti and white kurta and wears a turban on his head. The Manipuri bride does not wear too much heavy jewellery. This is surprising because Manipur is also known as the 'land of jewels'. The few basic ornaments that the Manipuri bride wears are a nose ring, bangles and earrings. The groom wears almost no jewellery.

## Manipuri Wedding Rituals

The Manipuris have a lot of fun during their wedding celebrations. First there's the *hinaba* ritual, when parents of both parties officially meet. If the horoscopes of the bride and the groom match, they fix the date of the wedding. Another pre-wedding ritual is the *yathangthanaga*, where the bride's parents visit the groom's place and consent to the wedding. The ritual of *waraipotpuba* is when the groom's family brings food to the bride's place. The engagement ceremony is called *Heijapot*.

Manipuri bride and groom

The groom and his family go to the bride's place on the day of the wedding. A Meitei woman welcomes them. The wedding altar and the seating arrangements are made around the *tulsi* (basil) plant. The bride and the groom exchange garlands and take seven circles (*saat pheras*) around the basil plant. *Kirtans* and the *shehnai* play in the background. Then two women from both sides release a pair of *taki* fish into the water, which symbolizes the bride and the groom.

At the end of the rituals, a grand feast is served to the deities for their blessing to the newlyweds. A Manipuri wedding typically ends with a custom called *manganichakouba*, which takes place five days after the wedding. This is to celebrate the newlyweds' first visit to the bride's family. There a grand feast awaits them.

Though dowry is not customary in Manipuri weddings, when the bride's parents bid her farewell, they give her essential household items like utensils and clothing.

A marriage procession in Manipuri tradition is called *jatra*

Manipuri wedding items

## AMAZING BODO MARRIAGE RITUALS

The Bodos of Assam follow the principles of Brahma Dharma, which do not allow the caste system or dowry to exist in their society. A common system of marriage flows through the tribal community in all Bodo villages. It is the village elders who select the bride. The bride price is paid to the groom's family to finalize the marriage. Bodos do not marry from other communities, and they also have a strict taboo against marriage within the same clan.

> The Bodos also have a ritualistic naming ceremony. After a Bodo baby is born, a cock is offered as a sacrifice to the gods for the welfare of the infant.

Sunday is considered the best day for a Bodo

wedding. The groom must stay with his bride's family for a few days after the marriage ceremony is concluded.

### The Bodos: An Introduction

The Bodo language belongs to the Tibeto-Burman lingual family, and although the Bodo tribe predominantly speaks the Bodo language today, in the early days, they used the Assamese and Roman scripts to communicate. The Bodos are the second linguistic group that entered Assam after the Austroasiatic. They predominantly live near the Brahmaputra Valley and are believed to be the first settlers of Assam. Historians believe that the original home of these tribes was in western China, near the Yangtze and the Huang He Rivers. These tribes are believed to have entered Myanmar from here and then India, following the course of the Brahmaputra, Chindwin and Irrawaddy Rivers. The Bodo tribe is also the first to cultivate rice and rear silkworms. Bodos love singing and dancing. Their dress sense is exquisite, and the women dress glamorously. Swarg-Aroi, Basumati-Aroi, Ramsa-Aroi, Mahalia-Aroi and Haj-Arois are different clans of the Bodo people.

## MIZORAM WEDDING CULTURE

The land of blue mountains, Mizoram, has a vibrant wedding culture and has recorded the most inter-caste marriages in India. The Mizo tribes follow the ritual of bride pricing, where money is paid by the groom's family to the bride's family. The boy approaches the girl's family to settle this bride price.

The liberal Mizos permit an extended courtship period for the would-be couple, which is followed by the engagement. Most Mizo weddings take place in church. The bride usually wears a white gown, a symbol of purity, but some brides prefer to wear their traditional dress, called *puanchei*, at their weddings. The bride covers her hair with a veil and holds a bouquet of flowers in her hand.

The groom wears a black suit. The bride gives a *puandum* (a traditional rug) to the groom. It is the same rug that is used to wrap the body of the groom when he dies – till death do us part!

## THE BIG FAT BENGALI WEDDING

A Bengali wedding is a grand affair that is a culmination of artistic and traditional beauty and celebrations. The sacred rituals are an integral part of Bengali weddings and bind the entire celebration. What also makes these rituals unique is that they consist of two different sets of rules (*niyam*) depending on which part of Bengal they originate from. The Ghotis are Bengalis native to West Bengal, while the Bangals trace their roots to erstwhile East Bengal before the partition, now known as Bangladesh. The fun element and the entertainment quotient are heightened in the event that the groom is Ghoti and the bride is Bangal, or vice versa. Both parties try their best to have their rules followed in the rituals, which adds to the fun. The weddings are also a foodie's delight as the cuisine on offer is the best of both worlds.

## Pre-wedding Rituals

- **Aashirbaad**: The pre-wedding ceremonies begin with the *aashirbaad* or *sagai* – the engagement ceremony, which is attended by the families of both the bride and the groom. The aashirbaad takes place before the actual wedding. However, in recent times, the aashirbaad is organized just before the wedding ceremony for the convenience of the guests. All the family elders and close friends bless the would-be couple with some *dhaan*, or rice grains, *durba*, or three-pronged grass blades, and delicious sweets. This is similar to *sagais*, a pre-wedding ceremony common in north India.
- **Shree Making**: A day before the wedding, the bride's family is seen making *shree*, which is nothing but a symbol of Goddess Lakshmi, the Hindu deity of wealth and prosperity. Married women in the family first take a tray woven with bamboo fibres. This is rounded from one side. Then they prepare a dough of rice on it in the shape of a pyramid. This dough and the tray are decorated with auspicious ingredients like turmeric, or *haldi*, and vermillion, or *sindoor*. For elasticity, a dash of mustard oil is added.
- **Nandimukh**: The day before the wedding, the ritual of *nandimukh* is performed at the groom's and the bride's homes by their respective families to pay tributes to deceased ancestors. The priest performs a puja, following which the holy spirits are invoked to bless the couple. After that, a fun element comes into play in the form of the last bachelor lunch for the bride

and the groom in their respective households. This ritual is called *aaiburobhaat*. *Aiburo* means 'bachelor', and *bhaat* means 'rice'.

- **The Haldi Ceremony**: The first ritual on the day of the wedding is the *dodhi mangal*, or the daybreak meal. The bride and the groom are supposed to eat only *chida*, or soaked flattened rice, mixed with sweet curd, or *mishti doi*. Then they are supposed to fast till they are married. The bride is also given a pair of white conch shells and red lac bangles called *shakhapola*, which, along with *sindoor*, are the symbols of a married Bengali woman. The *gaye holud*, or *haldi* ceremony, is conducted in the homes of the bride and the groom on the morning of the wedding day. Turmeric paste is first applied on the groom's body in a ceremonious ritual by seven married women of the household. The turmeric paste is believed to exfoliate the skin and brighten it. It is also supposed to bring good luck and ward off evil spirits. Then the turmeric paste is sent to the bride's house, accompanied by a collection of gifts called *tattva*, which includes saris and other apparel for the bride and her family members along with beauty

*Gaye holud*

products, footwear and other accessories. The most auspicious part of the tattva is a fish that is packed artistically along with the other gifts. A part of the haldi is applied on the bride by seven married ladies of her household as they circumambulate the bride, often while singing songs.

## Wedding Rituals

- **Samprodan and Saptapadi:** *Samprodan* (*kanyadaan*) means 'giving away of the bride'. This event takes place at the bride's residence or an outside venue arranged by the bride's family. Two representatives from the bride's family, usually the bride's uncle and her brother, pick up the groom from his house. The groom is accompanied to the venue by an uncle or elder brother known as *borkorta*. They are greeted at the entrance by women from the bride's family, who welcome him with *baron dala* as part of the *bor boron*, or welcoming the groom ritual. The groom is then escorted to the wedding *mandap*, and during the ritual of *shubhodrishti*, the bride is carried to the *mandap* by her brothers on a wooden stool. Her face is covered with betel leaves so that the groom cannot see it. At an auspicious moment, the bride uncovers her face, and their eyes meet to create shubhodrishti to the sound of ululation by the women and conch shells blowing in the background. Right after this, the ritual of *malabadol*, or the exchange of garlands, takes place between the bride and the groom.

  *Saptapadi* refers to the marriage vows and the seven rounds taken by the groom and bride around the sacred fire, which is a witness to seal their union. Saptapadi and samprodan are the two major wedding rituals of a Bengali marriage. The wedding rituals end with the sindoor daan, where the groom applies sindoor on the bride's forehead. The bride's face is covered after this with a new sari offered by the groom's family.

## Post-wedding Ceremonies

- **Baashor**: The first night after the wedding ceremonies conclude is called the *baashor*, where the groom and bride are kept awake by the bride's younger relatives, especially her siblings and cousins. This is more common among Ghotis, not so much among Bangals. The fun part is that the groom is denied entry by the bride's sisters till he pays them a hefty amount after a lot of haggling. Cut to the next morning when the *bidaai* ceremony takes place, when the bride leaves her father's home for her husband's. It is quite an emotional moment for the bride as she leaves her old home for a new one.
- **Welcoming the Bride at the Groom's House**: The bride's arrival begins the second wave of celebrations in terms of traditional post-wedding rituals. The bride is welcomed as she crosses the threshold of the home with her feet dipped in a mixture of *alta*, or *mahawar* (a synthetic dye also known as rose Bengal), and milk. Alta is a red dye made from the extracts of a plant named lac. In Bengali culture, alta symbolizes both Goddess Lakshmi and is applied all around the edges of the feet of women during auspicious occasions.

Milk is considered a symbol of prosperity and health across Indian culture. The bride is given cash gifts and gold ornaments. To make her comfortable in her new home, fun games are organized.

- **Boubhaat**: The *boubhaat* is the final ritual in a Bengali wedding and is the bride's feast. It begins with a lunch ceremony where the bride feeds the members of the groom's family with rice and other dishes. However, the bigger event takes place in the evening when the bride's family members, the groom's extended family, as well as guests are invited by the groom's family for a grand dinner. One day before the boubhaat, the bride's family gets tattva, this time for the groom and his family. Another post-wedding ritual is the bhaat *kapor* (rice and clothes) ceremony. The husband hands his wife a gift tray containing a new sari, sindoor and a plate full of food and promises to take the responsibility of providing her food and clothes from that day onwards. The bride is given a *loha*, or an iron bangle, by the groom's mother to be worn on the left wrist. The last post-wedding ritual is *phool shajya*, when the bedroom of the groom and bride is decorated with flowers for the couple to spend their first night together.

## THE CREATIVE TATTVA

Bengalis are an artistic lot, and decorating the tattva is where their creativity is unleashed fully. The bride and the groom's family members try to outdo each other in making the tattva special, not in terms of wealth but in ingenuity.

It's not uncommon to see the groom's dhoti folded in the shape of Lord Ganesha or the bride's sari folded in the shape of a butterfly. All the gifts are packed in beautifully decorated trays with coloured paper. Limericks and small poems sometimes accompany these gifts for the person they are intended for to create a few laughs.

## THE ANTI-DOWRY TRIBE

Unique to the culture of the Toto tribe of Bengal is the concept of monogamy and being strong opposers of the dowry system. After the death of his wife, a man is allowed to marry his deceased wife's younger sister. However, a woman is not permitted to marry her deceased husband's brother. One of the oldest traditions of a Toto marriage is to give a new name to the couple on the day of the wedding. Toto couples usually establish a separate household after marriage, adjacent to the paternal house.

### Toto Amazing Facts

The Totos are a small aboriginal Indo-Bhutanese tribe who live in the small village of Totopara, located in Alipurduar District of West Bengal. This tribe is anthropologically a branch of the Tibetan-Mongoloid ethnic group. The Totos are not only one of the oldest

Dhaniram Toto

tribes in the world but also one of the smallest, with a population of just 1,632, comprising 848 men and 784 women. There are 310 families in total in Totopara. Dhaniram Toto is a well respected personality among the Toto community. He has presented their unique language script to the people of India and recently received the prestigious Padma Shri Award for his outstanding achievements.

## THE TRIPURA TRIBAL MARRIAGE SYSTEM

The traditional Tripuri marriage system is called *hamjwktubuikaimani*. This system involves ancient customs of negotiations between the families of the bride and the groom, aided by a marriage broker and observed mostly among the Tripuris of the Sadar South. The marriage broker is called *raibai*, who plays an important role by paying a visit, along with the boy's parents, to the girl's home to select a bride. Several superstitions are religiously followed during this selection process. For example, hearing the bleat of a deer is considered a bad omen and so is the sight of a corpse. If they have a strange dream of falling out of their hut because of a cyclone the night before they set out for the would-be bride's place, the visit is cancelled the next day, probably because of impending cyclonic weather.

Traditionally, Tripuri society did not have a dowry system. With time, dowry became common. With or without dowry, today the next stage is a blessing ceremony day, called the *koksungma* (*mangalacharan*).

On the day of the wedding, the boy's family gathers in the home of the girl. The parents of the boy and girl sit next to each other, and two rice beer pots are kept before them. Two earthen oil lamps are placed beside these rice beer pots. A bell metal plate with some cotton, durba, copper coins, sesame seeds and soil is kept before both sets of parents so that the rituals of *dangdua* can be performed. Each person performs this ritual three times, and this is followed by the consumption of rice beer. The father of the bride pays for the meat to be had for the feast later. The would-be bride is fetched, who bows before her parents, prospective in-laws and other senior family members. The elderly people then bless the bride with money, coins or jewellery, and these articles are kept on the bell metal plate. After this, the bride has to bathe her parents and her would-be in-laws. In Tripuri custom, the bride also has to wash the hands of all the elderly people after they have finished eating. These rituals are known as koksungma, which solemnize the marriage.

The day before the wedding, women cut betel leaves and nuts with the names of the bride and groom. 'Ulu', a form of ululation, three times for the bride and seven times for the groom, is then heard, and all these form the part of the ritual called *kuaitano*.

On the morning of the wedding day, they worship the Lampra Wathop deity. The groom's family leaves for the bride's house with *jharie*s, or water pots, a palanquin and musical instruments. This is known as *khumphunugo*. After the wedding rituals conclude, the bride steps into the palanquin to leave her parents' home and travel to her in-laws' home. By Tripuri rules, the bride's mother cannot attend her daughter's marriage. She not only can't go to the wedding but she shouldn't be seen near her daughter when the latter leaves for the in-laws' place after the wedding.

The Tripuris keep dried turmeric, dice, *haritaki* (Indian walnut) and wild beans on a plate for the bride and groom to play dice. These games help break the ice between the bride and groom.

Tripuri marriages also have this interesting ritual where the groom's family offers wine bottles to the bride's family. The newly-wed couple is not allowed to sleep together on the first night, and this *kalratri* custom may have been borrowed from Bengali marriages. The next morning, the bride is taken for a bath. The wedding clothes are washed and stored away. New vessels are brought out for the bride to cook her first rice meal in her new home. The groom's family sets up a *bedi*, or marriage stage, and the bride and groom exchange garlands here. After this, the groom takes his wife inside his home. An artificial cradle is made, and a grindstone is kept inside the home to symbolize a newborn baby. The bride swings the cradle three times. All the guests and relatives have a good time singing, feasting and playing games. Drinks are served with traditional Tripuri cuisine. Sadly, this authentic Tripuri marriage custom is losing popularity in today's modern times.

## Wedding Attire

The wedding attires of Tripura are specially created by weaving and embroidery for the big occasion. *Rinai*, the bride's traditional wedding dress, is a long gown-type dress that is draped along the waist. The *risa* is also worn, which is shorter than the rinai. The colourful risa covers the chest and is a fine example of ethnic Tripuri fashion. The highlights of the risa are elegantly woven designs, floral patterns and brocade embroidery. The groom is clad in a dhoti and shirt. He also wears a waistcoat or sleeveless coat, made from the same material as the risa, over the shirt.

### Tripura: An Overview

Tripura features around nineteen major tribes. The largest indigenous tribe in the state is Tripuri, of Indo-Mongoloid origin who communicate in the Kok-Borok dialect. Tripura merged with the Indian dominion only in 1949 and was previously ruled by the Hindu Tripuri kings. The Tripuris are devotees of both Vaishnavism and the Shakti cult of Hinduism. Reang is the second-largest tribal community in Tripura and one of the seventy-five primitive Indian tribes. It is believed that the Reangs migrated to Tripura from the Shan state of upper Burma (present-day Myanmar). Other major tribes are the Jamatia, Chakma and Halam.

## THE EXOGAMOUS DHARUA

The Dharua society of Odisha has exogamous clan units, meaning that this tribe does not allow people from the same clan to marry. The two types of marriage that exist among the Dharua are the *curca* and the *tika* (union). In a curca marriage, a bride price is paid, and in a tika marriage, a divorced or widowed person is married or a Dharua marries someone belonging to either a higher or lower ethnic group.

### The Dharua Tribe: A Brief Overview

The Dharua are also called Parji and are a subgroup of the Gond tribe, which is the largest Indian tribal group. Today the Dharua live mainly in the central-eastern part of Bastar District and parts of Odisha, particularly the regions south of the Indrawati River. A large part of Dharua land comprises densely wooded forests and hills, with rivers and streams flowing into the valleys.

## THE BRIDE KIDNAPPERS OF LADAKH

For the Changpas of Ladakh, weddings are a never-ending party with endless feasting and drinking. The Changpas plan their marriages well in advance – as early as two to three years. However, in some cases, marriages are hastily arranged, keeping matters a secret to avoid *namaketches*, or the kidnapping of the bride. Bride-kidnapping marriages are not common but do take place occasionally. This type of marriage is unique to the culture of the Changpas. Thankfully, the girl who is kidnapped is not bound to oblige and ultimately gets to choose her husband.

## BHAGORIA MARRIAGE FESTIVAL

Looking for love and a perfect life partner? Welcome to Bhagoria. This harvest festival is celebrated by the Bhils and the Bhilalas of Madhya Pradesh, and this also serves as a tribal matchmaking live platform of sorts. The rules of the rituals are pretty simple. If a guy likes a girl, all he has to do is smear *gulaal*, or coloured powder, on her cheeks. If the girl reciprocates in the same way, the marriage is fixed. But, if the girl does not, the boy has to look for more gulaal and other cheeks. However, the boy gets another shot at winning the girl's heart after being refused once. If the girl applies gulaal on the boy's cheeks too, the couple elopes

Bhagoria Festival

before returning to be joined in a traditional ceremony in the village. This mass wedding ritual is pretty progressive by tribal traditions as it allows a couple to mix freely before marriage without family or social interference. Bhagoria is held in the West Nimar and Jhabua districts of Madhya Pradesh for about ten days just before the spring festival of Holi and is a unique festival for sure.

## THE KORKUS OF MADHYA PRADESH

A Korku boy is married off between the ages of eighteen and twenty-four, and a Korku girl gets married when she is between sixteen and twenty years of age. The parents and relatives decide on the marriage alliance, and a negotiator is sent on their behalf to the bride's house to negotiate the bride price and finalize the marriage date. The *gonam*, or bride price, that the father of the bridegroom has to pay the father of the bride is also frozen by the negotiator. The engagement party takes place in the bride's house, and the bride price is partially handed out during this ceremony. A male goat is killed and suffices as dinner for the entire village and the groom's party. The Korkus' weddings extend over a long period – even stretching to a year – because of the sheer expenses involved.

They start preparing for the marriage on a Wednesday, when the ritualistic bathing of the groom by his relatives takes place. The mother and other women of the family go to worship a deity called Muthwa Deo. The *bhumka* (religious leader) offers kumkum, turmeric, rice and coconut to Muthwa Deo. After returning home, the women apply turmeric paste on the groom's body. Molasses and liquor are distributed, and there is music, song and dance throughout the night to celebrate. Thursday morning sees the marriage booth being erected under the *patel*'s (village chief's) instructions. Four holes are dug where *supari* (areca nut), some money, kumkum and turmeric are placed. The holes are then filled with bamboo poles, and the booth is decorated with *jamun* leaves.

The Korku society is liberal in some cases, though, as both males and females are allowed to marry more than one person. A woman may also leave her husband and marry someone else. Social restrictions are not barriers to marrying someone within the Korku community.

## MUNDA MARRIAGE RITUALS: JHARKHAND

The Mundas do not marry members of the Santhal tribe and Ho tribes. But their marriage with the Oraon tribe is common. The Mundas also do not allow marriage between people belonging to the same caste. The marriage ceremony begins with the reading of omens. A scout is sent ahead of the bridegroom's party when it travels to the would-be bride's village. This is done to check for any inauspicious obstacles on the way, like spotting a black cat, which delays the journey further. The procession stops at the first mango tree they see, where the would-be groom's mother blesses her son. The procession is received on the outskirts of the village by the relatives of the would-be bride with songs and drumbeats. At the would-be-bride's house, the guests' feet are washed, and rice beer is served to them. Goats are also sacrificed, and then the bride price is settled. The final marriage contract is made by the embrace of the members of the *munda* community from the bride and bridegroom's side and the *pahan*s (the village priests) belonging to the two villages, which solidifies the union.

## KODAVA WEDDING DANCES

The marriage ritual of the Kodavas of Karnataka is one of a kind. They don't have a priest to conduct the marriage ceremony; the elders perform all the rituals. The sacred lamp with Lord Cauvery's picture is considered by the Kodavas as the sole witness to a wedding. The people of the community gather for the wedding feast after the rituals are completed. There, guests dance and perform the rituals of Ganga puja to music played by a local band.

### KODAVA/COORG WEDDING RITUALS

Currently, a traditional Coorg wedding in Karnataka is a two-day affair that may sometimes carry over to the early hours of the morning of the third day, which is perfectly understandable. The first day is called *urkooduva* (village gathering) or *karik muripa*, which mainly involves preparations for the wedding day. The second day is the wedding day, called *mangala*. On the first day, all present family members, both close and distant, actively participate in the wedding rituals. A representative of every clan, or *okka*, in that administrative unit, known as *nad*, participates in the wedding preparations. This person is instrumental in accompanying the groom to bring the bride home. On the first day, a pandal is built and decorated with mango leaves and bunches of bananas. There's a fifth post made of a sap-excreting tree, which supports the entire structure, topped by a canopy made of young jackfruit tree leaves or wild litchi branches and leaves. A mediator is present throughout the two days. Called the *aruva*, he plays a vital role by mediating between the bride and groom. He also supervises the preparation of the grand feast that takes place the night before the wedding. He oversees erecting the fifth and main *khamba*, or post, of the pandal. During the evening of the first day, a small party is thrown for close friends and relatives, where alcohol and several varieties of meat are served. Pork and alcohol are a must in a Kodava wedding feast.

A brahmin presides over the marriage ceremony, which happens at sunset. A cloth is held together by the couple, and as the sun sets, the cloth is removed and the couple holds hands. Then the couple walks seven times around a stone slab surrounded by four plough yokes.

### Kodava: A Brief Overview

The Kodavas of Coorg could be one of the earliest inhabitants of Karnataka. Kodavas have been hunters and warriors right from ancient times. They are a land-owning tribe who have strong ties to their marital tradition and land.

The Kodava tribe has exogamous septs. A man cannot marry a girl of his own sept or the daughter of his maternal uncle. Girls are normally married off at an early age.

## KOKNA MARRIAGE RITUALS

Among the Koknas, the engagement ceremony before the marriage is important. Here, the groom's family makes a demand of the bride's family, known as *penbharu*. The engagement is called *nanipan*, but if it does not translate into marriage, it is called *moti* pan.

On the day of engagement, the day of the marriage is frozen upon along with the kind of give and take, number of guests attending and so on. There are no child marriages among the Koknas, but they prefer cross-cousin marriages. The marriage proposal is always extended by the boy's father, and if accepted, the *bolpen* ceremony is performed, which is considered the betrothal. The marriage festival begins with the application of haldi paste on the boy and girl. The marriage party travels for the wedding in a truck, tempo or tractor to reach the bride's place in the morning itself. There is dancing and celebrations to the tune of musical instruments. The bride arrives at the wedding venue seated on the shoulder of a strong relative. The guests are offered strong refreshments like liquor, *tadi* (toddy) and bidi. The saptapadi ritual was performed by married women of the society earlier but is the domain of a brahmin these days. To celebrate the union, a sweet dish is served. The marriage party leaves in the evening after the day is mutually agreed upon for the bride's return for a few days.

Divorce can be granted also on the grounds of infidelity or various forms on incompatibility.

### The Kokna Tattoos

Members of the Kokna tribe, hailing from the coastal regions of Gujarat, Maharashtra, and Dadra and Nagar Haveli, love getting ink done just as much as they love their ornaments. Their favourite tattoos are those of gods like Rama, Hanuman and Krishna. According to the Koknas, tattoos enhance their physical beauty.

## MARRYING A MANGO TREE

The Dharua tribe of Odisha believes in arranged marriage. However, instead of consuming the king of fruits, the ritual of marrying a mango tree first is preferred to ward off evil spirits. They adhere to the rule of patrilocal residence after marriage and the patrilineal rule of descent.

### The Bride and Groom Kidnappers

The Shompen tribe, hailing from the Andaman and Nicobar Islands, has fewer women as compared to men. As a result of this sex ratio, many men have no partners. But marriage here is done by capturing men and women from various subgroups. As bizarre as it sounds, this ritual is part of their tradition, and they embrace it fully to date.

## BHEHULI BIYA: THE MARRIAGE OF THE FROGS IN ASSAM

This strange marriage ritual among the farming communities of Assam has the objective of bringing about a bountiful harvest through rainfall as local legend states that frogs tend to croak loudly to successfully announce rain. Perhaps it is assumed that marriage will make frogs croak in happiness rather than pain to usher in much-needed rainfall.

> A few communities in Uttar Pradesh, Maharashtra and Tripura also celebrate this unique wedding ritual, which just goes to show that amidst all the diversity in India, some things are also a constant.

The ritual is called *bhehulibiya*. This wedding is serious business, though, with the groom and bride dressed up just like humans as Vedic mantras are chanted by the priest and Vedic rituals are performed. Women sing wedding songs and guests are welcomed with food and drink.

## MARRIAGE OF HUMANS WITH ANIMALS FOR EXORCISM

Humans marrying animals is an age-old ritual in India that's been mentioned in the epic Mahabharata, when the *mangalik* princess Gandhari was married to a goat before she married the blind king Dhritarashtra. This strange ritual continues to date in parts of rural India when mostly young girls are married to a dog or goat to supposedly exorcise the spirits that are believed to possess them or if they suffer from any kind of deformity.

## PUNJABI WEDDING RITUALS

From Bhatinda to Birmingham, Punjabi weddings are a grand affair characterized by colourful celebrations, song and dance, and community participation. Punjab's rich cultural heritage comes alive in a boisterous mélange of dance, music, and rituals to create an ambience of warmth, happiness, hospitality and togetherness.

### Pre-wedding Rituals

- **Roka and Thaka:** The official engagement is announced at the *roka* ceremony, which is also the formal announcement of the wedding alliance. At a close gathering of the bride and groom's families, sweets, gifts and blessings are exchanged. The *thaka* ceremony follows the roka as a *mauli*, or sacred thread, is tied around the groom's wrist. This symbol of protection symbolizes that the groom is accepted into the bride's family. Similarly, jewellery is offered to the bride from the groom's family in order to solidify the alliance.
- **Sagan:** This may take place months after the roka at the opportune moment that is calculated by the priests. In the *sagan* ceremony, a puja is done for the groom which is conducted by the bride's father and brother.

On the other hand, the bride is presented with a special decorated *chunni* from the groom's family. This is to signify that both the families formally accept and welcome the bride and groom as their family member and bless the union. This is also the event when the engagement rings are exchanged by the couple.

- **Sangeet:** During this celebration of music and dance, friends and family gather for the upcoming wedding. The Sangeet sees their song and dance performances in full flow and the Giddha and Bhangra traditional dances are the icing on the cake and the most popular choice, however, performances on Bollywood songs are also popular. Folk songs centred on the theme of marriage are sung as part of tradition.
- **Mehndi Ceremony:** During the mehndi ceremony, the hands and feet of the bride are decorated with beautiful henna designs. This ritual is supposed to usher in prosperity and good luck, and henna is applied on the hands of the female guests as well. The name of the groom is hidden in the design of the bride's mehndi as a ritual so that post the wedding the groom has to spend time finding it. Traditionally, the name of the bride is also written on the groom's hand.
- **Jago:** This pre-wedding ceremony witnesses the family and friends of the bride and groom gathering together to spread the news of the wedding and celebrating.

## ON THAT DAY

- **Haldi/Maiyan Ceremony:** In this cleansing and beautifying ritual, haldi is applied to the bodies of both the bride and the groom. The ritual is also a symbol of protection and good fortune. This takes place on the day of the wedding.

- **Chooda/Kalire Ceremony:** This act signifies the transition of the woman from a maiden life into married life. The *chooda*, a set of traditionally red bangles, is given to the bride by her uncle (mother's brother) to signify blessings from the maternal side. Traditionally, it is to be worn for at least a year's time and removing it is a ritual in itself. *Kaliras* are metallic ornaments tied to the *chooda* by the bride's sisters and friends. As part of the ritual, all the friends and sisters who are eligible for marriage are lined up and the bride tries to break a piece of the *kalira* on them. If a piece falls, it is said that they would get married next. In the same ceremony, a traditional red thread called *gana* is tied to the wrists and ankles of the bride and groom to protect them from all negativity on the wedding day. The *gana* usually consists of betel nuts, a piece of iron, *ghungroo*s, *kaudi* and other metal rings. This is tied with seven knots and for fun, the bride and groom are tasked to remove each other's *gana* after the wedding.
- **Gharoli/Ghara Ceremony:** In this traditional ceremony, a decorated pitcher of water from a nearby temple is fetched by the siblings of the bride and the groom. This symbolizes the beginning of their journey as husband and wife.
- **Sehrabandi:** In this traditional ceremony, a decorated veil is tied to the forehead of the groom by his sisters, mother or other female relatives, and a small puja is done. The sisters then feed the horse that is to take

the groom to the venue. A younger cousin or nephew is dressed up like the groom, as the *sarbala*, who sits with the groom on the horse and is believed to be a protector of the groom on the day.

- **Baraat:** The groom's procession is called the *baraat*, which is a grand and colourful event. The groom's choice of transport is usually a decorated female horse, or *ghodi*, which he rides or a decorated vehicle. Once the Baarat reaches the venue, they are welcomed with some puja and some rituals. The mother of the bride tries to pinch the nose of the groom before entering the venue and the groom has to prevent it. This is done to establish a playful relationship between the bride's family and the groom.
- **Milni:** This is the meet-and-greet ceremony where the families of the bride and groom exchange blessings after meeting. This takes place only among the male members of the families.
- **Varmala:** The couple seal their union and commitment towards each other by the ritual of exchanging garlands.
- **Joota Chhupai:** The groom's sisters/sisters-in-law hide his shoes playfully in this light-hearted and fun ritual and return them only after a certain amount is paid up by the groom.
- **Kanyadan:** The father of the bride gives her hand to the groom, and this ritual of kanyadan symbolizes the transfer of responsibility.
- **Mangal Phera:** The bride and groom take the seven vows by circling the sacred fire seven times to seal their commitment and love for each other.

- **Anand Karaj:** The Sikh wedding ceremony is called Anand Karaj, and this takes place in the Sikh temple or the Gurudwara. The couple is seated before the Sikh holy scripture, the Guru Granth Sahib, and the Granthi or the priest presides over the wedding ceremony, which comprises the reading of hymns, *laavan* (the exchange of vows) and the tying of the Sikh wedding knot called the Anand Karaj knot. The couple walks around the Guru Granth Sahib four times to solidify their commitment towards each other.

## Post-wedding Rituals

- **Doli and Vidaai:** The bride bids her family members goodbye as she travels to her husband's home traditionally in a *doli*, or palanquin (these days a decorated car).
- **Grah Pravesh:** The bride and groom reach the threshold of their marital house, and a puja is performed to ward off any evil before they enter into their new life. The bride lightly kicks on a *kalash* full of rice symbolizing her role as Lakshmi and to bring abundance and prosperity into their lives. She dips her feet in red *aalta* and walks inside the house, taking the first steps towards the temple at home.
- **Kangna Ceremony:** In this post-wedding ritual, the rings of the bride and groom are

The ring hunt

dropped in a platter of milk and water. The couple is asked to find the rings and this is symbolic of their new life as a couple.

- **Pag Phera:** The bride and groom visit the bride's paternal home as a married couple just the next day.

## PRE-WEDDING RITUAL OF INDIAN CHRISTIANS

Like Hindu weddings, haldi ceremony is common in Christian weddings too, especially in North India. In Goa they also apply coconut paste on the bride- and groom-to-be. In some places, this pre-wedding Christian ritual is called the Roce ceremony.

Wedding rings and a wedding saree used at a Christian wedding in Kerala

## HERE ARE SOME WEDDING RITUALS COMMON IN MOST PARTS OF INDIA

Haldi is one such pre-wedding ceremony of India that is common among many communities, including Hindus, Muslims, Christians and Sikhs. It is also called vatna or mayian in Sikh tradition.

Pheras, usually seven, taken by the bride and groom circling the sacred fire

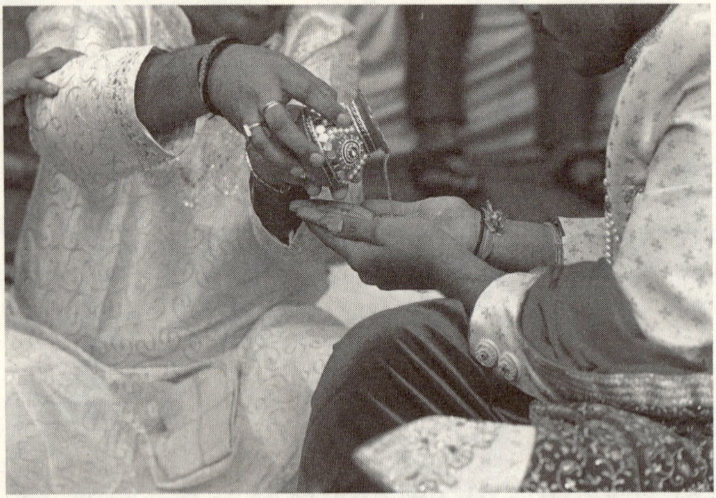

Kanyadan: this ritual symbolizes the transfer of responsibility of the bride from the father to the groom (today this is considered regressive by some people)

Indian Hindu groom applying vermillion in the parting of the bride's hair

Mehndi is a common ritual in Indian wedding, both for Hindus and Muslims. Henna is applied to the hands and feet of the bride.

Nikah ceremony in a Muslim weding is the main ritual that formalizes a marriage with the consent of both the bride and the groom in the presence of a kazi and witnesses.

## HOW MUCH MONEY DO YOU HAVE?

Who can forget Steffi Graf's epic reply when a fan proposed to her during a Wimbledon semi-final in 1996: 'How much money do you have?' Now, did Andre Agassi have to wear a garland like this to win her heart?

A Hindu groom wearing a garland of currency notes is a common sight in North India. Occasionally, extravagant shows of such garlands hit the headlines.

# 2

# MUSIC AND DANCE

Through music, we can connect with the divine and experience the transcendental.

– ***Pandit Ravi Shankar***

## THE WHISTLING TRIBE OF MEGHALAYA

Meghalaya's Kongthong village in the East Khasi Hills is located 56 km from Shillong. The villagers have a unique ritual to identify their tribe members, which has become a tradition. They sing instead of speaking when they address someone. The villagers use a unique form of whistled identity instead of names, which has earned them the moniker 'the Whistling Tribe of Meghalaya'!

Every time a baby is born, the mother composes a distinct melody inspired by nature, and this lullaby becomes a distinctive identity of the child for life. The personal sound could be inspired by the call of the birds, the rustling of the leaves or anything else that is in sync with nature. Amazingly, this lullaby has no words and is just a kind of humming that only the villagers are able to recognize and remember. Only the title of the lullaby, which is about five to six seconds long, is used by the villagers to call out to each other instead of calling each other by name, and this is known as *jingrwai lawbei*, meaning whistling lullaby. The whistling tribe of Meghalaya never repeats a tune, and amazingly, no two tunes are alike, just like a fingerprint or the stripes of a zebra. This melodious tune is introduced by the mother to the infant, who begins responding to it. Soon it is used to communicate instead of just using a name. This practice has been employed for generations now. When a person dies, the tune that was used to call him is not given to anybody else.

### THE WHISTLING VILLAGE

Kongthong has a population of 650–700, and thanks to their unique whistling communication, there has been a widespread interest in this hamlet. The main positive has been the construction of a motorable road that has enhanced connectivity with Kongthong, which could earlier be accessed only after an 8–10 km trek. In 2021, Kongthong was selected for entry to the 'Best Tourism Village' by the United Nations World Tourism Organization (UNWTO), thus showcasing its cultural importance and potential for sustainable tourism. The whistling tribe is deeply connected to the environment, and each tune reflects the best of nature's rhythms, thus giving the remote Kongthong an unparalleled cultural identity. Whistle on!

## AMAZING DANCES OF THE KHASI OF MEGHALAYA

### Dances with Swords

Unmarried girls, dressed resplendently in their traditional costumes, dance alongside men. The male dancers hold a sword in their right hand and normally a white yak hair whisk in their left hand when they dance vigorously. They keep time to the accompanying music of the changing beats of drums and the *tangmuri*, or pipes, that play in the background.

### Ka Shad Suk Mynsiem

This annual spring dance celebrates the harvest and sowing seasons. Men and women are dressed in colourful clothes and jewellery during the dance performance. However, only unmarried girls can participate in the dance. Men are not allowed!

### Doregata Dance

At the Doregata Festival, women try to knock off the turbans of their male partners using their heads as they dance. The simple reward is laughter if the women succeed! Off with his head!

## Pomelo Dance

This solo dance, called Chambil Mesara, demands great skill. The performer ties a cord to his waist and attaches a pomelo to the same. Then the dancer swings it around without moving the hips. Some expert dancers can use two separate pieces of fruit hanging from the same cord. This is a custom followed in the A'song Festival.

## Lahoo Dance

Both males and females participate in the lahoo dance, performed at the Behdienkhlam Festival. Dancers are dressed in their best dance costumes. Two young men are usually positioned on either side of a woman, and they hold arms while dancing. The usual drum and pipe are replaced by a cheerleader, a man good at impromptu recitation, and he recites unplanned couplets to the delight of the audience. This ritual is believed to ward off the demon of cholera or plague.

## Wangala

Wangala is also called the 'Dance of the Hundred Drum Festival', an important festival for the people of the Garo Hills. It lasts for a week every year in November, ending a period of hard labour to yield a bountiful harvest. The festival and dance honours Satyong, the god of fertility, for blessing the people with a good harvest. Young and old alike are dressed in their beautiful costumes and feathered headdresses as they dance rhythmically to the beat of long, cylindrical drums.

### Mangona or Chugana

Mangona is a post-funeral ceremony of the Garos. The guests are served pork and beef after the funeral rites of the dead. Singing and dancing take place for the entire night as the funeral dirge, known as *kalee* or *mangtata* (*grapmechia*), is chanted.

## AMAZING MANIPURI DANCE FORMS

In Manipur, dance is considered not just an art form but a key component of Manipuri culture and life. It is a form of natural expression that's deeply woven into the social fabric of the state and its inhabitants. Manipuri dance is a completely religious art form with the intent to create a spiritual experience, where entertainment is the secondary motive. Dance is a form of worship and enjoyment, opening the door to the divine. It is also a key element of all the Manipuri sociocultural ceremonies. No wonder that dance is treated by Manipuris with great reverence.

Manipuri legend states that Lai Guru Sidaba created the earth and also created seven Laibangthous (gods) and seven Lainuras (goddesses). These celestial beings were supreme dancers and levelled the uneven surface of the earth with their divine dance steps. Thanks to a holistic approach, Manipuri dance has percolated from generation to generation like water through a sieve thanks to the *guru–shishya parampara*. Apart from the intricacies of dance movements, students are also taught important lessons on the values of life.

Traditional Manipuri dance is certainly diverse. The local indigenous creation story is enacted by priestesses through a dance ritual. Next comes the ancient martial art form of Thang-Ta, presented through a ritualistic dance. There is also the raasleela, a dance form that depicts the story of Lord Krishna and his *gopi*s. Then there are the male-dominated dance forms, which are performed with practised ease and are accompanied by traditional musical instruments like percussion and cymbals. This dance performance is witnessed during ceremonies like childbirth, marriage and bereavement. There are also several folk dance forms performed at different festivals throughout the year. All the dance forms, irrespective of genres like folk, classical or modern, are devotional in nature. Moreover, the folk dances of Manipur are a sight to behold because of the exotic costumes the dancers are dressed in, as well as the simple but graceful rhythms observed in the dance movements. It's amazing how Manipuri folk dance can be ritualistic, entertaining, religious and worldly at the same time. The major folk dance forms include:

## Lai Haraoba

*Lai Haraoba* means 'the festival of gods'. This dance form enacts how the universe was created according to local ancient beliefs. Traditionally, Lai Haraoba is performed at village temples before the shrines of Umanglai, the ancestral god of the Meiteis. *Maiba*s (priests) and *maibi*s (priestesses) perform this to invoke the deity.

The unique aspects of the life and philosophy of the Meitei people are highlighted in this dance. This pre-Vaishnavite legacy of the local culture makes the shrines of the ancestral forefathers, called *laibung*s, buzz with festivity during the Manipuri New Year. This is when people also do penance for their sins and make New Year's resolutions.

This ritualistic dance is considered the predecessor to the classical Manipuri dance form.

Women performing at Lai Haraoba

## Thougal Jagoi Laisam Jagoi

Men and women dancers worship the deity by dancing before it to bring about an auspicious beginning to the ritualistic duties performed that day. The dance ends on a funny note as a tug of war between the men and women takes place. The dance has been stylized for stage presentations in recent times.

## Kanglei Haraoba

According to Manipuri legend, Khoriphaba, the son of Laviningthou Soraren, the lord of heaven, was enchanted by the beauty of the earth. He saw Thanjing, Marjing, Wangbren and Konbru, the ancestral gods who were responsible for guarding the four corners of the earth, dancing together. Khoriphaba asked the gods if he could join in, but the gods refused as he had no partner. But they later allowed him to choose a partner from amongst the gods' divine daughters, who were part of the audience. Khoriphaba was blindfolded and made to choose his partner with a stick, or *kangjei kaghu*. Then he joined the dance with his partner. This tradition of *lai nupi thiba*, which means 'god's search for a consort or partner', continues to date and is performed by priestesses now.

## Pao-Sa Jagoi

This dance is part of the traditional Kanglei Haraoba. *Pao-sa* means 'conversation'. Legend says Nongpok Panthoibi (goddess of civilization, birth and death) set out in search of Nongpok Ningthou (the ruling guardian deity of the eastern direction). She reached Nongmai-Ching, a hillock, where she met Nongpok Ningthou. After their union, they had a conversation where they recalled memorable incidents of their past life and celebrated by singing and dancing.

## Kabui Dance

The Kabuis, or Kabui Nagas, live in the western hill ranges of Manipur. They boast of a rich tradition of dance and music. Dressed in their exquisite traditional costumes during the Gang-Ngai Festival, the Kabuis perform a series of dances in different stylized forms. Heavy drums and high-pitched songs make for a perfect accompaniment. The boys hold sharp weapons called *dao*s in their hands and dance around in circles along with the girls. Shim Lam and the Kit Lam are some of the famous dances of the Kabui Nagas. Shim Lam is also known as the Fly Dance. Kabui legend states that a prophet named Mhung created the laws pertinent to all living creatures on earth. Mhung performed a sacrifice called *jourunei*, in which he invited all the creatures, and each species performed their own dance at this sacrificial ritual. In Shim Lam, people follow moves that are believed to be originally performed by Tajuibon, a flying insect with shiny wings. The dance replicates the movement of the insect as it flutters from one flower to another to drink the sweet nectar. The dance is a main part of the Gang-Ngai Festival. Kit Lam is a colourful harvest dance performed by the Kabuis.

## Katabenlu Laam Kabui

The katabenlu laam, meaning 'bangle dance', consists of intricate footwork and pulsating movements.

## Takin Taremlaam Kabui

This dance is also performed at the Gang-Ngai Festival held in January. The Kabuis pay homage to their ancestors and worship the spirits of the home and hearth through this dance.

## Mao Naga Dance

The Mao Naga people live in the northern mountains of Manipur. As part of the annual harvesting and seed-sowing festival called Chikhuni, the young population of the tribe display intricate footwork and graceful movements when they perform the Mao Naga dance. Then there is the Mao Maram dance (*Asharali Odo*), consisting of vibrant and rhythmic yet smooth movements, which is another popular dance of the Mao Nagas that is performed ritualistically.

## Luivat Pheizak Dance

The Luivat Pheizak dance is performed by the Thangkhul Naga community of Manipur during traditional festivals. It depicts the various stages of cultivation and the simple lifestyle of the community. However, there are no musical accompaniments, except for quadruple tones or notes of different pitches, during this dance.

## Thang-Ta

The art of Thang-Ta displays the wonderful technique of combat, Manipuri martial art, using the *thang* (sword) and the *ta* (spear). It was mandatory for all Manipuri men to go through intensive training to master this art so that they were prepared for war. This dance gives basic training in warfare and enhances physical strength, speed and agility of the mind. The kings of Manipur loved this dance form and kept Thang-Ta experts in their courts. All the dance movements of the Meiteis are believed to have their origins in this martial art. The dance movements of the Thang are also believed to keep evil spirits at bay. The martial arts practised by Meiteis include sword fighting, spear fighting and wrestling. A Thang-Ta performance begins with *Khurumjaba*, a ritual meant to invoke the

Lord and seek blessing from the god as well as the gurus and the audience.

Here are the different variations of the Thang-Ta:

### Thang-Chungoi Yannaba

Themed on a duel, in this dance the Teo warriors carry a sword and a shield. The shield is called *chungoi*.

### Ta-Kousaba

This art form has been taught for generations and is performed in an open area, where the dancers use spears. This spear dance has nine different steps, which are called *khausaral*. This dance can be seen at the Kwak Jatia and Lai-Haraoba Festivals where dancers with a *chung*, or long shield, and a spear, gyrate like a warrior.

### Thang-Ta-Chaieraba

This pre-Hindu ritualistic dance is a duel between the sword and the spear, wielded by each warrior dancer. However, the dancer carrying a sword is armed with a shield but the one with a spear lacks a shield. The dancer with the spear performs *khousabai*. These are steps aligned to the rules of Khausarals – nine types of martial steps seen as the basics in Manipuri dance. The steps the swordsmen display are known as *thanghairol*.

### Yet-Thang Oi-Thang Yannaba

This dance involves great dexterity, as each dancer handles two swords simultaneously. This martial art form was mainly used in battles but has been stylized for stage presentations today. This can be witnessed during royal functions and at the Lai Haraoba Festival.

### Thang Leiteng Haiba

This is decorated swordplay and is performed by highly skilled swordsmen. The choreography of this dance merges martial arts steps with masters of the sword.

### Thang Amaga Aniga Yanaba

A man armed with two swords fights two men simultaneously, and these two warrior dancers hold a sword and a spear respectively. This dance has the same rules and principles as thanghairol.

### Chei Khatpa

For this one needs sticks – one long and two shorter ones. It is derived from an indigenous Manipuri game called *cheitek kotpi.*

### Meibul-Thang-Ta

This martial arts dance uses the *thang-leiteng*, or sword movement, and *ta-khousaba*, or spear movement. However, firesticks replace the two weapons in this fire dance, which is a visual treat.

### Lhou Sha

This war dance is performed at every confrontation between two villages. It is part of the tradition of the Maring community of Manipur and is also performed to conclude important festivals. It was initially performed by men only, but its evolution into a folk art has ensured that women participate with equal fervour.

## Dhol Dholak Cholom

The festival of colours, Holi, is called *Yaoshang* in Manipur. It is not surprising that the festival witnesses devotional songs and dances. Vaishnavism, or the worship of Lord Vishnu, is popular in Manipuri culture. As a result, *sankirtan*, or the worship of Lord Krishna and Radha through music and dance, is also a popular Manipuri ritual, especially during festivals. *Dhol dholak cholom* is performed during Yaoshang, and the dhol, the dholak and a variety of drums serve as musical accompaniments for the popular dance form. The drummers are dressed in colourful costumes. They play a range of rhythms and perform acrobatic feats simultaneously, which is a grand spectacle of skill, grace drumming and fire play.

> *Dhol dholak cholom* means 'singing and dancing to the tune of the drums dhol and dholak'.

## Pung Cholom

Another popular dance during Holi or Yaoshang is pung cholom. *Pung* is the Manipuri drum, which is the heart and soul of this dance. A series of rhythmic patterns are played on this musical drum, and the drummer also dances to his own tunes through footwork and body movements. The pung cholom is part of the music of the *sankirtan* tradition as a musical tribute to Krishna and Radha and is hailed as one of the best art forms of Manipur.

### Pena Cholom

The *pena*, a stringed musical instrument, is also played during sankirtan. It is played during the dance called pena cholom, where the dancers move gracefully as they play the pena.

### Mandil Nartan

Mandil nartan is a dance that is performed during the festival of Jhulan Yatra in Manipur. Here, the dancers dance to the tune of small cymbals called *mandila*, which they play themselves. The mandil nartan dance is a depiction of Radha and Krishna on the *jhula*, or swing, as they are flocked by the *sakhi*s, or girlfriends, who dance around them.

### Khubak Ishei

The chariot festival, or rathayatra, in Manipur witnesses this unique festival dance called khubak ishei, where the song of Dashavatar is performed while the artistes clap their hands as musical accompaniment to the dance. This dance displays the *tandava* aspect of Manipuri dance. Tandava is Lord Shiva's dance of cosmic destruction.

### Raas

Raas is a dance drama with the theme of the union of Lord Krishna with his female devotees, known as *gopi*s, and particularly, his consort and devotee Radha. This unique Manipuri dance has been labelled the 'jewel dance' from the land of jewels. The dance also reflects the rich Vaishnavite tradition of Manipur. The themes of the dance centre on Krishna leela, or the different episodes from young Krishna's life. One must not miss the *vasant raas*, one of the leelas, celebrated on Chaitra Purnima, or the full moon night in the month of Chaitra (April–May). The dance symbolizes the eternal love of Radha and Krishna. The rich costumes worn by the dancers add to the grand spectacle. The dance concludes with an aarti, a ceremonial worship of the holy union of Radha and Krishna. Raas leela was first visualized by Maharaja Jay Singh in the eighteenth century.

> Various episodes from the life of Radha and Krishna are the most dominant themes of dance forms in Manipur.

Manipuri raas leela

## THE FLAUTISTS AND DRUMMERS

The Angami Nagas of Nagaland are fond of music, and they use flutes and drums to create tunes and rhymes.

They follow a culture where the love of music is passed from one generation to the next. They are also famous for their traditional dance – circling a bonfire while live music is being played.

### Angami Nagas

The majority of Angami Nagas live in Kohima, which is divided into four regions. In the north region, Agamis live in villages of North Kohima and Dimapur District. In the south, they live in the foothills of Mt Japfu. The rest of them live in the west and east portions of Kohima.

## DANCE FORMS OF MIZORAM

Mizoram's natural splendour is complemented by most visually captivating dance forms. The diverse and unique Mizoram dance forms are delightful to watch. These group dances reflect the jubilant spirit of the Mizos and are often seen at Mizo festivals.

### Cheraw

Cheraw, or the bamboo dance, is the major traditional dance form of Mizoram. This visually striking dance is also one of the oldest dances here. Long bamboo staves play a key part in this fast-paced dance form. Six to eight people sit face to face on the ground, holding the bamboo sticks. They open and close pairs of horizontal and cross bamboo staves in sync with the rhythmic beats of gongs and drums, and the dancers move in and out of this pattern of bamboo sticks. Performed with great care and precision, Cheraw is also the most popular Mizo dance.

Women performing Cheraw

## Khuallam

Khuallam is the dance of the guests who are invited from other villages. Gongs called *darbu* are the musical instruments played during this dance. This dance does not have any songs as musical accompaniment. The guests wrap the traditional handwoven Mizo cloths around their shoulders and dance by swaying the fabric.

## Chailam

Chailam is performed during the Chapar Kut Festival in Mizoram. Men and women stand in a circle, and the men hold the shoulders of the women while the women hold the men's waists. The musicians are right in the middle of the circle. They play the drums and *mithun* horns to accompany the dance.

Mithun horns

## Sarlamkai

Sarlamkai is a traditional dance form and one of the oldest in Mizoram. It has been performed as a celebratory dance after victory in a war since olden days. Men and women stand in their places, while the hero dances as he holds his shield and his sword, swinging it to the accompaniment of gong beats.

### Mizoram

The remote north-eastern state of Mizoram is called the songbird of the north-east. Mizoram has about fourteen scheduled tribes, like the Mizo, Chakma, Pawi, Kuki, Lusha, Ralte, Lai and Hmar among others. Each tribe is diverse and distinctive, reflective of their historical immigration patterns. According to local folklore, the Mizos came out from under a large rock covering called Chhinlung. Historians, however, are of the view that Chhinlung is a reference to an ancient Chinese city in the Yunnan Province of China. They think the Mizos migrated to the Chin Hills in Myanmar from here around the thirteenth century BCE before they came to present-day Mizoram.

## THE BELL DANCE

The main festival celebrated by the Abhuj Maria tribe of Chhattisgarh is called Kaksar, which is held in June. Kaksar is the local deity, as well as a group dance. The bell dance is performed by young boys and girls. Tinkling bells of different sizes are tied to the waists of the dancers, and they jingle-jangle with the dance movements. These bell sounds have a soothing effect enhancing the accompanying music.

## THE VANISHING HALLAKI AND THE SINGING RITUAL

Northern Karnataka's picturesque Ankola town houses the primordial Hallaki Vokkaliga tribe. *Hallaki* literally means 'milk' (*haalu*) and 'rice' (*akki*) in Kannada. This tribe is diminishing alarmingly, often believed to be a result of exposure to urban lifestyles. The new generation of the Hallakis is fast-embracing the trends of rapid modernization. A sincere attempt to save the rituals and culture can however be seen too.

The Hallaki women sing about everything, from their little secrets to protesting about issues in their daily lives, right from the people they met in the past to the ones they are likely to meet in the future. Their poetic songs probably originated as a cure for boredom and to kill time as the Hallaki women kept each other company by singing as they journeyed deep into the forests and hills to fetch log firewood or ploughed through the wide paddy fields. The unwritten accounts of detailed Hallaki rituals are also sung as songs.

## GARBA AND DANDIYA

Garba and Dandiya are dance rituals inspired by Indian mythology and are common during Navaratri. These traditional dance forms of Gujarat have become popular not only in India but also across the world. In Garba,

Garba

Dandiya

people, traditionally women, move in a circular pattern with rhythmic hand and foot movements. This dance ritual performed in the honour of Goddess Durga celebrates fertility and womanhood. Dandiya is performed in pairs, with decorated sticks in hand. The movements reflect a mock-fight between Goddess Durga and the demon Mahishasura.

## TRIBAL EPICS

When Hallaki women sing the stories of the Indian epics, the Ramayana and the Mahabharata, the narrative is definitely surprising to say the least. The Hallakis call the Mahabharata the Pandavara Kami and the Ramayana the Seethe Kami. One version of the tribal Ramayana glorifies Sita more than Rama. Also, as a departure from the original epics, the Seethe Kami is much longer than the Pandavara Kami and has to be sung for the whole night.

The Hallaki women are also experts in natural herbal medicines.

The Hallakis were originally hunters and used the skin of the monitor lizard to make their unique drum called *gumte*, an instrument used majorly during their annual harvesting festival dance. New instruments are in fashion now that hunting has been deemed illegal. Even traditional costumes lack what used to be essential once, peacock feathers.

### Origin of the Name Hallaki

The origin of the name Hallaki is still unclear. However, a local legend has it that Lord Shiva was ploughing the field once when Goddess Parvati tripped and fell while carrying food for her husband. Rice and milk fell on the mud together. Parvati created a male and female doll out of that muddy mix and returned home. Lord Shiva left his ploughing and went home to look for Parvati. He saw the dolls instead, and when he touched them, they sprang to life as the Hallakis.

The dolls reportedly told Lord Shiva, 'We came to life because you touched us. Now tell us what we should do for a living.'

Shiva said, 'You were born when I was ploughing the field, so you will continue my work.'

Therefore, agriculture became the main occupation for the Hallakis. Because they came to life thanks to a mixture of muddy rice and milk, they were given the name Hallaki (see above what *haalu* and *akki* mean). But, according to the *Bombay Gazetteer*, they got the name Hallaki because they grew rice that was as white as milk. Obviously, the Hallakis prefer to go with the tale of Lord Shiva.

## TRIBAL DANCE: THE DHAMAL OF THE AFRICAN-INDIANS

Nestled in the depths of Gujarat is the picturesque village of Sirvan, where the Siddis live. They are an unusual tribal community with an ancient African origin. Although the Siddis can't claim to have retained their African heritage, language or history, the one thing they have held on to from their precious African lineage is the passion for music and dance. The Siddis are reputed for their Dhamal dance, part of a rich and unique musical tradition. This expressive dance form portrays the community life of the Siddis and how they have managed to survive in the forests for so many years.

The women of the Siddi tribe wear saris and a range of ornaments while performing the Dhamal. Saffron and acacia leaves are tied on the waist and wrists and worn as headgear by the members of the community. Then they stick peacock feathers to the headgear – a sort of finishing touch. The culture of the Siddis is brought to life through their costumes. Their faces are also painted, using colours extracted from natural dyes. The women dancers highlight their devotion to their god as they perform, singing a repetitive song pattern, while the men play the *dammam*, a musical instrument made of wood with deerskin on the sides. Dhamal was known as Mashira Nritya in ancient times and reflects the Siddi passion for hunting. The Siddis usually performed this dance after returning from a successful hunting campaign. During the rule of kings, Dhamal was the main source of entertainment in royal courts.

### Out of Africa: Tracing the Origin of the Siddis

Historians believe the origin of the Siddi population can be traced to the Bantu people of south-east Africa, who were brought to the Indian subcontinent as slaves. Most of these Bantu migrants converted to Islam, while a small part of the population became Hindus. It is to be noted that the nizam of Hyderabad also had African-origin guards and soldiers in his employ.

Family of African origin Siddis at Sasan, Gujarat

It is often believed that the Siddis were brought to India from Africa as slaves by the Portuguese on behalf of the nawab of Junagadh. However, the ancestors of the Siddis were first brought to India as slaves by Arabs as early as the seventh century, much before the Portuguese did so. Then there were others who came to India on their own accord. These were not slaves but free people who travelled to India as merchants, sailors and mercenaries and stayed on before the Portuguese slave trade escalated matters. When slavery was abolished in the eighteenth and nineteenth centuries, the Siddis spread into the thick jungles.

These people were earlier called Habshis, which is a Persian word for Abyssinian (Ethiopia was earlier known as Abyssinia). But only the ones who rose through the ranks in the royal court were honoured with the title Siddi, which is a likely etymon from the Arabic word for master, or *sayed/sayyid*. It is however not recorded when the term *Habshi* was replaced by *Siddi*. Today the term *Siddi* is used to describe all types of people of African descent in India. The Siddis worship nature, believing that spirits are present everywhere in nature, like rocks, trees, rivers and mountains. The Siddi people believe that these evil spirits must be appeased, or they can cause the eventual downfall of the Siddis by unleashing natural disasters upon them.

## THE KOKNA DANCING MASK

The Kokna dancing mask is a fearsome-looking one for sure. The mask is worn during dance performances by members of the Kokna tribe. The stylized face wears a tiered crown, and tiny circular eye holes are cut out in the eyes to help the dancer navigate with the mask on. Masks are carved by the artisans of the tribe to represent mythological characters for the Bhavada Festival, which is a unique blend of dance and drama, celebrated in March and April. The masks were earlier carved from softwood, which allowed for extensive detailing when it came to various facial expressions that are key in a dance drama. Now modern masks are in vogue, made from papier mâché as they are lighter and more durable. The characters represented by these unique masks are either deities like Vishnu, Ravana and Ganesha or ancestral spirits, totems, other mythological characters, animals and birds. Each dancer dances to the tune of musical instruments like the *sur*, *kahali* and *sambal*, mimicking his character to perfection through dance. During the festival procession, masked dancers enact myths from tribal folklore as well as Hindu epics like the Ramayana and Mahabharata.

A moment from the Kokna Festival

## THE MUSICAL SANTHALS

The vibrant Santhal culture features a mélange of music, dance, art and oral traditions. The Baha dance and Soor Diul Festival are integral to Santhal identity and highlight their strong bond with nature and agricultural practices. The Santhals are also famous for their skill in pottery, making musical instruments like the *tirio* and traditional Santhal paintings.

### Santhals: An Overview

The Santhal are the largest of the tribal populations in South Asia, spread across West Bengal, Assam, Jharkhand and Odisha. Their origins are believed to be the Champa Kingdom of Northern Cambodia, and they lived a nomadic life in the past. Found predominantly in Bihar, the roots of this courageous and creative tribe date back to the pre-Aryan period. The word Santhal is derived from two words: *santha* meaning 'calm' and peaceful and *ala* meaning 'man'. But behind that calm and peaceful demeanour, Santhals are also renowned for being great fighters and fought the British in the war for Indian independence. A heroic Santhal named Sidhu is believed to have accumulated ten thousand Santhals and formed a parallel government to challenge British rule. However, it was Baba Tilka Majhi who was the first Santhal to fight against the British, in 1784. Organizing the Santhals, he formed an armed group to counter the British acts of exploitation and resource grabbing.

## A SONG FOR EVERYTHING

The Konyak tribe of Nagaland does not have any written script. All communication of their history, traditions, culture and knowledge have been transmitted orally from generation to generation through folklore, folk songs, poems and general sayings about the ways of life. The Konyak tribe loves to sing, and there are songs for every daily chore, no matter how mundane, including tasks like farming or rice pounding. Oral lores about daily life, love, death, headhunting and tattooing dominate the life of the Konyaks.

## KATHAK RITUALS

Kathak is a vibrant classical dance form which originated in Uttar Pradesh. Kathak features important rituals like *vandana* which is basically an invocation where the dancers pay homage to their guru and musicians. Kathak also has the use of greetings by the dancers like Nakaskaar or Salaam based on the Hindu or Muslim tradition.

## AMAZING RITUALS OF DANCES FROM SOUTH INDIA

The rituals of Kathakali, a classical dance-drama form from Kerala, embraces rituals through elaborate make-up, detailed costumes and symbolic hand gestures called *mudras*. The ritualistic angle of Kathakali also goes with the theme of the triumph of good over evil and the dance-drama narrates famous stories from the epics and Hindu mythology.

Another dance form from Kerala called Theyyam originates from tribal rituals. The costumes and masks worn by the dancers are symbolic of the tribal deities and spirits.

Padayani is a dance ritual with its roots in Central Kerala. The dancers wear colourful costumes and masks as they engage in this dance to celebrate a good harvest. The dance movements of Lord Shiva are replicated by the dancers, which are made to appease Goddess Durga.

The *Bhoota Kola* or *Bhoota Aradhne* is a ritualistic dance form. This annual ritual featuring spirit worship is practised in both Kerala and Karnataka. The name is derived from the Kannada words *bhoota*, meaning 'ghost' or 'spirit', and *kola*, meaning 'play'.

Bharatnatyam is a classical dance form with its roots in Tamil Nadu. Bharatnatyam is a blend of devotion and skill and is renowned for both aspects. The spiritual aspect highlights the devout prayer and the cosmic connection between the dancer devotee and God. The rituals of Bharatnatyam include the offering of flowers to the divine called *pushpanjali*, the rhythmic invocation through *Alarippu*, and the addition of melody to dance movement through *Jatiswaram*.

The Karakam dance from Tamil Nadu is performed during the annual festival before the idol of Mariyammai. The objective is to pray to the goddess of pestilence so that she does not unleash a pandemic on the people during the year.

## ODISHA DANCE RITUALS

The Odissi dance from the state of Odisha has its roots firmly fixed in ancient temple rituals. It features rituals like *Mangalacharan*, or the auspicious ceremony, *Batu/ Sthayee* or establishing the core movements and elements of Odissi, *Pallavi*, which is abstract dance with decorative detail, and *Abhinay*, a or dramatic representation. All these rituals blend together beautifully to narrate stories and express emotions through Odissi.

Odissi dance

# 3

# FESTIVAL RITUALS

For the wise man, every day is a festival.

– ***Plutarch***

## THE RITUALS OF THE NONGKREM DANCE FESTIVAL

The *pomblang* goat-sacrifice ritual is performed by the *syiem* of the Khyrim, the administrative head of the Hima or the Khasi State, in the company of the high priest. Oblation is offered to Lei Shyllong, the deity of Shillong Peak, by sacrificing a goat or a rooster. After this sacrifice, offerings are made to the ancestor and ancestress of the ruling clan. The Nongkrem dance festival is annually celebrated during autumn, normally in November, at Smit, the cultural centre of the Khasi Hills, which is about 1 km from Shillong. This festival is a five-day-long extravaganza performed to appease the all-powerful goddess Ka Blei Synshar for a bountiful harvest and to ensure the peace and prosperity of the Khasis. Mostly unmarried people take part in the dancing ritual.

## FESTIVALS OF THE KONYAK TRIBE OF NAGALAND

The Konyak tribe has festivals throughout the year. Any important event is incomplete without a feast in the village. The main festival is the annual Aoling Festival, which is also called Aoleang Monyu, and takes place in the beginning of April. This spring festival welcomes the spring season and also celebrates the new sowing season. The Konyaks pray to their supreme god, Wangwan, for a rich harvest and also remember the ones among them who have passed away. The ritual sees the erection of a bamboo with branches, with tender palm leaves hanging in the front. After this, the spirits of the ancestors are praised and invoked. The Konyaks meet old friends and family members during this festival and also make new friends. Not a single village goes without celebrations. People feast merrily, sing folk songs and dance to the beat of long drums. Everyone is dressed in their traditional attire. Competitions are organized with prizes for the winners. The Konyak men wear their traditional clothes, and their famous headdresses adorned with hornbill feathers and boar tusks. Men also sport brass skull necklaces around their necks. Their attire is perfect for performing their war dance. The festival attracts visitors from all over the north-east, and each day of this special festival has a special significance. The Aoleang Monyu Festival is also a time for feasting as food and drinks is indulged in aplenty. Apart from the wide variety of ethnic cuisine on offer, a vast quantity of rice beer is brewed and consumed.

- Day 1: This day sees the weaving of traditional fabric, the making of rice beer, the collection of wood and vegetables, a chicken sacrifice and the prediction of the future by astrologers.
- Day 2 and 3: Training in hunting is given to young boys.
- Day 4, 5 and 6: Celebrations are held with food and drink, indigenous sports, games, music and dance.

## NAAG PANCHAMI: THE FESTIVAL OF SNAKES

The festival of Naag Panchami is held across India. Live cobras with their venomous fangs, instead of deities, are worshipped by devotees. The rituals of the festival of snakes involve the sprinkling of turmeric-vermillion powder and flower petals over the raised heads of cobras. Then the snakes indulge in a sumptuous meal of milk, rice and even rats sometimes. It is claimed that the origins of this festival are rooted in Hindu mythology when Lord Krishna fought a dreaded, monstrous snake called Kalia. After defeating Kalia in battle, Lord Krishna blessed the snake that it would be worshipped by people on this day and fed milk. The festival of snakes is celebrated by humans on the fifth day of the Hindu month of Shravan. This period extends from the first day of the full moon at the end of July and stretches to the third week of August on the day the next full moon appears.

## FESTIVALS OF MIZORAM

### MIM KUT

The months of August and September witness this important festival of Mizoram. This vibrant extravaganza features song and dance for four to five days. This is primarily a maize festival that pays homage and tribute to the ancestors of the Mizos by offering bread, vegetables and maize, of course, among other items.

### CHAPCHAR KUT

Chapchar Kut is considered the oldest festival of Mizoram. Farmers cut down bamboo forests partially to create space for seasonal farming. After the bamboo heaps dry up, they are burned. Mizo people turn up in their traditional clothes. They also sport amazing hats made from parrot feathers and beads. At the festival, one can see a very special ritual in which the men sit on the ground and beat each other with bamboo sticks as they sing traditional songs while the women dance with graceful movements.

### Pawl Kut

Pawl Kut is held in December to celebrate the harvest of straw and is a thanksgiving festival. Meat and egg are a must-have at the festival feast while rice beer is consumed heartily.

### Thalfavang Kut

November sees the festival of Thalfavang Kut, which ushers in the harvest season. Cultural events like games are also a part of this festival. After the sporting activities, a feast is mandatory. Tribes and communities pitch in their respective collections to enjoy a sumptuous celebration.

## PABARANA PURNIMA: THE VIRTUOUS FESTIVAL OF THE CHAKMA TRIBE

The Buddhists of the Chakma tribe of Tripura celebrate a unique festival called Pabarana Purnima on the full moon night after Dussehra, or Vijaya Dashami. Their Hindu counterparts celebrate Lakshmi Puja at the same time, which is called Hojagiri in Kokborok. The Chakma is one of the major tribes of Tripura. Biju is one of their most famous festivals and takes place during the harvesting season. In fact, Pabarana Purnima is of prime importance to the Buddhist Chakma tribes of Tripura as well as in the neighbouring state of Mizoram, where the Mog tribe celebrates this festival. The celebrations of the Chakma and Mog tribes are similar, with slight variations. The two underlying principles of Pabarana Purnima are *adopting wholly* and *forbidding*. The former means the practice of committing to Buddhist qualities like humility and simplicity. Forbidding, on the other hand, suggests giving up the ways of life that go against Buddhist principles. On Pabarana Purnima, the Chakmas and other Buddhist tribes recall this virtuous quality propagated by Gautama Buddha and immerse themselves in seeking and granting forgiveness. Forgiving someone is one of the most virtuous qualities in Buddhism and brings luck and blessings to the forgiver. The devotees begin this pious day by attending a prayer meeting organized by the Buddhist temple committee. This takes place in all the Buddhist villages, and the villagers get up early in the morning to bathe and dress up in their best clothes. They attend the puja, which begins at 9 a.m. and continues till noon. The presiding Buddhist monks perform the pujas. The Chakmas worship Lord Buddha, followed by the worship of *Shibuli/Sivali*, an *arhat*, or saint, held in high esteem by the Theravada Buddhists. Among the Chakma Buddhists, *Shibuli* is given the same seat of worship as Goddess Lakshmi is given by the Hindus. Shibuli is worshipped by the Chakmas to bring prosperity, fortune and well-being. The ritual of *Ashtapurashkar* follows the puja. This is all about donating clothes and other essential items to the monks. The important ritual of *Moitri Binimoy* is next, which *is* the act of seeking and granting forgiveness. After the rituals are over, the monks break for lunch. They have an early lunch as they are forbidden to consume any food that involves chewing after noon. So the villagers serve the monks lunch before noon and have lunch after the monks are done. After lunch, the rest of the day is all about the monks spreading the messages of the Buddha and teaching the principles of Buddhism in the villages.

## VARUNA YAJNA: MAHARASHTRA

India is mainly an agrarian economy, where most households depend on a good agricultural yield for their survival. Hence, rainfall is an essential element for survival as without it, there would simply be no food. The states of Maharashtra and some parts of Karnataka and Tamil Nadu witness a grand festival to appease the rain gods when the Varuna Yajna is performed. A series of purifying rituals are performed to please Varuna, the Hindu god of water. This is done every year before the monsoons begin in June. At first, a purifying fire is lit by the temple priests, who chant hymns in honour of Varuna. Then the priests immerse themselves in huge barrels of water and chant Lord Varuna's name one lakh times.

## DHINGA GAVAR: RAJASTHAN

Rajasthan is known for its colourful rituals and festivals. But Dhinga Gavar is certainly a unique pick. We've all seen parades and processions in festival rituals across the world. But what makes this one unusual is that only women dress up as different characters, like Hindu gods and goddesses, cops and robbers, priests and saints and several interesting characters during this procession. They carry idols of Goddess Parvati adorned with kilos of gold. The colourful characters are armed with lathis or heavy sticks to protect the 30 kilos of gold and large offerings of cannabis (at least traditionally, when it was not banned in India before 1985). Anyone trying to usurp these treasures, albeit playfully, receive a sound thrashing. This beating is, however, considered holy, especially if you are an unmarried man looking to tie the knot. The ritual takes its name from Gangaur, another name of Goddess Parvati. According to mythology, she had once playfully teased Lord Shiva by dressing up as a tribal woman. This playful side of Gangaur is called Gavar and has become an annual festival in Jodhpur, Rajasthan, which is celebrated on the occasion of Teej in July–August.

Dhinga Gavar

## DAHI HANDI: THE HUMAN PYRAMID OF MAHARASHTRA

The unique human pyramid, or Dahi Handi, is one of the popular rituals in Maharashtra on the festival of Janmashtami, the birthday of Lord Krishna. The human pyramid is formed by young men called Gokuls, with the objective of fetching the reward in a *handi*, or earthen pot, hanging at a huge height. The handi-breaking is achieved after long hours of practice. The reward contains fruits and dairy products like milk, curd, butter and ghee, as well as some cash. The prizes are sponsored by societies and brands. Music, dance and celebrations follow this festival dedicated to Lord Krishna's love for butter and dairy when he was a kid.

Dahi Handi

## GOVARDHAN PUJA: WORSHIPPING COWS

Cows are considered sacred in Hinduism. During Govardhan Puja, cows receive special treatment when they are worshipped and fed lovingly. The rituals of this puja include smearing turmeric and vermillion powder on the foreheads of cows and placing flower garlands on them. These rituals differ from region to region in India. But the festival normally takes place on the fourth day after Diwali in the month of Kartik in the Hindu calendar and begins with the new moon in November.

### Holy Cow!

A certain village in Maharashtra celebrates Govardhan Puja in the most unique way possible. In Bhiwdawad village, it is observed on the day of Ekadashi, which is a day after Diwali. This Ekadashi is also known as Dev Uthani Ekadashi or Prabodhini Ekadashi, which symbolizes the awakening of Lord Vishnu from his four-month slumber or Chaturmas in Hindu mythology. This auspicious day marks the beginning of the Hindu wedding season.

After the cows have had their ritualistic bath, they are decked out with flowers, coloured powder and henna. Then the villagers do something really strange. They lie down before the herd of cows and urge them to trample their bodies by walking over them. This is done to fulfil their *mannat*, or wish, after a five-day fast as the villagers believe the god will be appeased and grant their prayers after this act.

## AMBUBACHI MELA: HONOURING THE MENSTRUATING GODDESS

Sadly, menstruation is often seen as a subject that's still a taboo in India, and there have been reservations against allowing menstruating women into temples. That's what makes the Kamakhya Temple in the Assamese capital of Guwahati unique. It celebrates the menstrual cycle of

Kamakhya, the Hindu tantric goddess of desire. This annual festival is held in June for three days. Legend has it that when Lord Shiva performed the Tandava, holding the dead body of his wife Sati, parts of her body fell on earth. Each body part fell on a certain part of the earth to form a Shakti Peetha, and temples were built at those spots to honour Sati. Sati's *yoni*, or vagina, is believed to have fallen at the site of the Kamakhya Temple. During the three days of the festival, the temple doors are shut to visitors. It is believed that the temple turns red inside. The goddess supposedly makes this happen by menstruating for three days, during which the healing powers of the 'menses' of Mother Earth is available to all devotees. However, Kamakhya is not worshipped in the form of an idol in this temple but is a yoni-like stone with a natural spring flowing on top. The deity is dressed on all days in a red silk cloth called *rakta bastra*, or blood clothing. The deity is offered fruit and light offerings like flowers and sweets. The red cloth is considered auspicious by devotees, who tie pieces on their wrists on the fourth day when the temple reopens after the goddess has rested. Even outside the temple, the red is prominently displayed on flowers, vermillion and clothes as ascetics and Aghoris gather from all over the country to pay homage to the goddess and show off their psychic powers to interested devotees. This is because the origins of this festival are in the tantric Shakti cult.

> The Aghoris are sadhus who worship Shiva. They live an ascetic life and known to meditate on cremation grounds.

### THE DREADED AGHORIS

The Aghori Shaivite sadhus are certainly fearsome at first sight with their normally naked bodies smeared in ash and their long, matted hair. Found primarily in the holy city of Benaras and some parts of Uttarakhand, the dreaded Aghoris take part in shocking rituals like the consumption of human remains before or after dead bodies are cremated and sexual intercourse with corpses. It is believed that they possess healing powers for the living as well, which is the reason for their popularity. The spirits of the dead will disagree!

## THE SECOND MENSTRUATION CELEBRATION

Menstruation is also celebrated in Raja Praba, Odisha. But this festival correlates the fertility of a woman with that of the harvest. All agricultural work comes to a standstill for three days as Bhumi Devi, or Mother Earth, the wife of Lord Jagannath, menstruates as she undergoes the process of regeneration. Bhumi Devi receives a ceremonial bath from her human devotees on the fourth day of the festival. The celebration is a gala time for young girls and women, who dress up in their finest clothes and eat delicious food. They socialize for three days at a stretch to break free from their mundane routines.

## SHIGMOTSAV

The various communities of Goa boast of a rich tradition of art and culture, which is reflected in their festivals. Their songs and dances make the spring festival of Shigmotsav come alive in glorious colours. Held in February–March, the grand rituals and ceremonies of tribal Goa are prominent in this highly choreographed event. Shigmo is a farmers' festival that celebrates the arrival of fresh crop. The Shigmo Festival coincides with the last month of the Hindu calendar, which begins on Dashami and Holi. The village of Barcem in Goa celebrates with the beats of the dhol, *tashe* and *kassal* on the final day of Tonniocho Mell, a traditional celebration of Shigmo.

### The Bachelor Dance

The *Dinya Zatra* is a unique dance tradition of the Velip community of Goa. Celebrated during the Shigmo Festival, bachelors, or *Dinya*, dance before marriage holding sticks called *Dinnya boddio* as traditional music is played by dhols and tashas. This is a way for the Velip youth to celebrate their cultural traditions before marriage. The word *Dinya* is derived from *dindo*, meaning 'bachelor'.

The celebrations begin four days before the *Dinya Zatra* as all the young and old male members from the Velip community participate in a unique ritual. Leaving their homes in the village, the men walk through different villages, crossing several water bodies and forests barefoot. They perform from 8 a.m. to 8 p.m. in the front yards of village homes. After three days of strenuous performance, the villagers return to Barcem, where they assemble at a specially created open space called *maand*. The men dance around in a huge circle here, and they cannot return to their homes until they complete the dance. In fact, no dancer is allowed to leave the performance midway even if there is a death in the family. Although this seems a rather extreme form of dance, the rituals of this festival are so strong and deeply rooted that they follow the rituals no matter what. The dance is a sight to behold as the men dance with two uniform-sized bamboo sticks in a synchronized manner. Each dancing clan is composed of 150–200 people who perform at different houses. The newly-wed men sport a different headgear called *turo*, while the other men wear colourful headgear in shades of pink, orange and red. Some wear heavy anklets, which add a unique musical sound to the performance. The footwork is so precise and fast that one cannot miss a beat. The last part of the dance is performed with a lamp and the deity in complete silence as homage to the deity. After each performance, the men are offered a coconut and lunch or dinner.

### The Velips of the Deep Forest

The Shigmo Festival is celebrated a bit differently by the once forest-dwelling tribals called the Velips. Their religious and cultural life is mainly related to the forest. Earlier, the

Velips were totally reliant on the forest for food, fodder and fuel. Today, even though they are not reliant on the forest totally, this old ritual is still practised. The men of the tribal village leave their homes to enter the forest, leaving the women and children behind. They invoke local deities through folk songs and dances for two days, walking without footwear and consuming only vegetarian food in the deep forest.

The Velips are believed to be a sub-caste of the Kunbis. Their origins are claimed to date back to the Stone Age. The Velips occupy the Stone Age site that was discovered recently at Kajur, and they also practise a lifestyle similar to that of the pre-historic period. The name Velip refers to the ones whose ancestors settled in a Goan village. They are called 'Gaonkar' (Sanskrit – *gaon*: village). The surname 'Zarkar' comes from *zara*, which means 'fountain'. 'Dahikar'' is a surname derived from the word *dahi*, or yoghurt. The Velips live in a joint family system, and their economic condition is more stable than most other Indian tribes.

## DURGA PUJA: THE RIO CARNIVAL OF BENGAL

For Bengalis living in Bengal and outside, Durga Puja is the most-awaited festival of the year. Week-long festivities take place as the puja is performed both in traditional homes (*bonedi baadis*) and in public with structural decorations called pandals, where the idol is housed.

Various pandal themes and styles of the goddess are on full display as people throng in huge numbers to witness this extravaganza. Durga Puja is enhanced by scripture recitations, performance arts, entertainment, feasting, visits to family, gift-giving and carnivals. Bengalis believe that during this auspicious occasion, Goddess Durga descends on earth, which is her parental home, from her bridal home in Mount Kailash, accompanied by her children, Ganesha, Kartikkeya, Saraswati and Lakshmi. The idols depict Goddess Durga and her children on their respective mounts in a grand spectacle. Several rituals are witnessed during the five days of Durga Puja, beginning with *Shoshti*, or the sixth day of Navratri, followed by *Shaptami*, *Ashtami*, *Nabomi* (*Navami*) and *Dashami*, or Dussehra, which is the tenth day. Below are a few of the prominent rituals of Durga Puja.

- ***Bodhon:*** On Shoshti, the first day of Durga Puja, the goddess is invoked through the Bodhon ceremony in the evening. This stems from the belief that Lord Rama began this worship to seek Goddess Durga's help in defeating Ravana in battle. Before this, other rituals take place, like promising the goddess that all the rituals will be performed according to the norms of Durga Puja.
- ***Nabapatrika Snan:*** In this ritual, nine plants, including the prominent banana plant, are tied to form the nabapatrika, or nine leaves, which symbolize the nine forms of Shakti or feminine power. The nine leaves are Brahmani (banana), Kalika (colocasia), Durga (turmeric), Kartiki (*jayanti*), Shiva (wood apple), Raktadantika (pomegranate), Sokrahita

(*ashoka*), Chamunda (arum) and Lakshmi (paddy). Nabapatrika is taken for a *snan*, or ritualistic bath, in the river Ganga on Shaptami, or the seventh day. She is then wrapped in a traditional sari and placed next to Lord Ganesha as his *kola bou*, or banana bride. The name is derived from the banana leaves, which are the most prominent among the nine leaves.

- ***Pushpanjali:*** The floral offering made to the goddess by devotees with cupped palms under the guidance of a priest chanting mantras is called pushpanjali or anjali. Anjali is offered from Shoshti through Dashami, but Ashtami's anjali is considered the most special. The auspicious hour is announced beforehand. The devotees fast and wear clean clothes, often new, after a bath to be able to perform this ritual. They repeat the mantras after the priest, holding flowers with bel leaves in their cupped hands, which are offered to the goddess after the mantras are chanted. Three rounds of mantras and floral offerings take place during pushpanjali.
- ***Kumari Pujo:*** The ritual of kumari pujo is held on Ashtami, the eighth day. A prepubescent girl is worshipped as the living incarnation of Goddess Durga at some places. She is decked in fine clothes and jewellery. One can see kumari pujo at Belur Math, the centre of the Ramakrishna Order founded by Swami Vivekananda.
- ***Sandhi Pujo:*** The ritual of sandhi pujo begins at the hour when Ashtami concludes and Nabomi begins. This symbolizes the time of the day when Goddess Durga appeared in her furious Chamunda form to slay

the powerful demons named Chanda and Munda. The ritual witnesses the lighting of as many as 108 lamps. As the priest chants the mantras, frenzied beats of the *dhaak*s accompany it. The ancient custom of sacrificing an animal has been abandoned now in most places, and vegetables are symbolically offered in its place.

- ***Dhunuchi Naach:*** On the evenings of Durga Puja, especially on the last two days, the fun-filled and entertaining dance ritual with the *dhunuchi* (a type of censer) takes place. Clay pots are stuffed with burning charcoal to create the dhunuchi, which people hold as they dance to the beat of the *dhaak*s. The expert dancers show off their skills by dancing with a dhunuchi in each hand, balancing the dhunuchi on their head or holding it by their teeth. Dhunuchi

Bengali women performing dhunuchi dance on the occasion of Durga Puja naach was earlier a male domain, but today, women participate with equal fervour.

- ***Sindur Khela:*** The ritual of Sindur Khela is held by married women before the goddess is taken for immersion in a river or any other water body. These women offer vermillion, the mark of a Hindu married woman, to the goddess along with an offering of sweets. Then these women apply vermillion, or sindoor, on each other's faces playfully.
- ***Bisarjan:*** The ritual of Bisarjan, or immersion, is when the idols of Goddess Durga and her children are taken out in a procession along with plenty of dancing and dhaak playing. This immersion in the river, which is quite a spectacle, marks Goddess Durga's return to Mount Kailash.
- ***Bijoya:*** The ritual of Bijoya marks the conclusion of the grand festival of Durga Puja. The young touch the feet of the elders and seek their blessings on the evening of Dashami. Men perform the act of *kolakuli*, a traditional gesture of hugging each other to increase male bonding. Special sweets are distributed, and people visit each other's homes for Bijoya.

## THE FESTIVAL FOR SONS-IN-LAW

While the rest of Bengal is busy preparing a grand welcome for Goddess Durga during Durga Puja, the members of the Toto tribe of West Bengal gear up to welcome their sons-in-law instead. The Totos observe a unique festival called Arsing at Tading Hill, situated on the India–Bhutan border, in Alipurduar District. The festival takes place on the Durga Puja days of Shaptami, Ashtami and Nabomi. The Arsing ritual focuses on welcoming and taking care of sons-in-law and begins after Mahalaya. Arsing strengthens the bond between two families. The festival is a much-anticipated part of the winter season, characterized by delicious food and the exchange of gifts among daughters, sons-in-law and children. The custom of this ritual is that the son-in-law sends *yu*, a local liquor made from a grain named *maroa*, to his in-laws through his wife. This indicates that the son-in-law will follow suit. Elaborate arrangements are made early in the morning to welcome the son-in-law. Pork dishes were an integral part of the Arsing spread for a son-in-law earlier. However, several health-conscious households have now replaced pork with chicken.

## NEEL PUJA

People in West Bengal also celebrate Neel Puja, or Neel Shoshti, on 13 April. The rituals are engaged in mostly by married women who fast throughout the day and break this fast after they have poured milk over the Shiva lingam at the Shiva temple. The aim is to obtain Lord Shiva's blessings for the welfare of the woman's children. The origin of this ritual is the marriage of Lord Shiva with Goddess Parvati. Shiva is Neel here. The name is derived from 'Neelkantha' or 'the one with the blue-coloured throat' in reference to the poison Lord Shiva gulped down to save the world from extermination in Indian mythology. A local deity named Shoshti is worshipped along with Lord Shiva. This goddess is a symbol of the betterment of women and their existing and unborn children. She is accompanied by a cat and six children, and the deity is made from the mashed paste of wet rice grains.

## MAHA KUMBH

The Maha Kumbh Mela held at Prayagraj, Uttar Pradesh, is one of the largest religious gatherings in the world. It is a wonderful amalgamation of faith, tradition and devotion. Millions of pilgrims and saints gather from across the world at the sacred rivers to participate in important rituals of Hinduism. The highlight is the *shahi snan*, or royal bath, which is performed by saints and key spiritual leaders. This holy dip at the confluence of the rivers the Ganga, Yamuna, and the mythical Saraswati – all considered sacred – is believed to wash away all sins and invoke divine blessings. The ritualistic bathing takes place on predetermined auspicious days with the objective being to purify oneself and attempt at liberation from the cycle of life and death to attain *moksha*. This spiritual experience is what draws devotees to the Kumbh in droves.

> The kumbh mela takes place every four years at Prayagraj (earlier known as Allahabad), Haridwar, Ujjain and Nasik – by rotation. Maha Kumbh takes places once in 144 years at Prayagraj.

Pilgrims at the Kumbh Mela

## THE BANESHWAR FAIR

The Bhils are South Asia's largest tribe and one of its oldest. This race of pre-Aryans has also been mentioned in both the Indian epics, the Ramayana and the Mahabharata. The Bhils are found in several Indian states but are predominant in Rajasthan. The Bhils of Rajasthan boast of a vibrant culture. The entertainment on offer includes a fascinating mélange of music, dance, craftsmanship and celebratory rituals and traditions. The Baneshwar Fair is the main festival of the Bhils and is an ode to Lord Shiva. The Bhils assemble on the banks of the Som and Mahi Rivers. They camp in the area, dancing to traditional songs around a blazing fire. This is topped up with cultural shows, magic shows, animal shows and acrobatic displays. But the icing on the cake is the most famous folk dance of the Bhils, the Ghoomar, which is an eye-catching display of grace, colour and movement.

## THE HATTI FESTIVAL OF BUDI DIYALI

Budi Diyali is a festival celebrated by the Hatti tribe exactly a month after Diwali on the *Amavasya* of *Maag-Sheersh* according to the Hindu calendar. People dance and sing holding fire-lit torches. The festival denotes the triumph of good over evil, the divine over dark forces and overcoming demons with light and fire. The mythological links to the three-day festival suggest that the celebrations are for Sita's return to Ayodhya after the *vanvaas*, or fourteen years of exile in the forest along with Rama and Lakshmana as narrated in the Ramayana. To mark Sita's return, the elder women of Ayodhya had decorated the city with fire torches. The festival is symbolic of the same celebration. Another explanation is that the fire-lit torches and the song and dance accompaniment depict the legendary battle between Indra, the lord of the Devas, and the dreaded *danava* Vritra.

Several regions of Kullu District in Himachal Pradesh celebrate a similar festival, where villagers perform a special dance popularly called *haathi nach*, or elephant dance. Dancers seek shelter under a large cloth canopy designed to resemble an elephant and dance in unison, imitating a warrior who is seated on the elephant. Specific positions are assigned to dancers according to the intra-community hierarchy. The Hatti community follows a rigid hierarchy and is divided into two categories. The powerful Bhat and Khash form the upper echelons of society, and the Badhois are below them in the pecking order. Marital alliances between these two categories are usually not encouraged. The Badhois take up the invisible positional duties and serve as the elephant's feet to carry the men of higher status on their backs. Men belonging to the upper category of the Hatti society perform the role of warriors in the dance drama, which depicts a war-like situation. Warriors are displayed fighting while riding the elephant. They make manoeuvres displaying sword movements with their ancestral swords and shields to display their bravery and skills in battle. The dance drama focuses only on the warriors, who are in the spotlight. The ones carrying them are hidden under the canopy with the suggestive shape of an elephant and decorated likewise. The performance is regal, entertaining, symbolic and grand. But the dark side also highlights discrimination and marginalization and the evils of inequality and social hierarchies prevalent in certain sections of Indian society.

### The Hatti Clans

There are two main Hatti clans in India. The first lives in the Trans-Giri area of Sirmaur District in Himachal Pradesh, and the second is found in Jaunsar Bawar of Uttarakhand. The traditions and rituals of the two Hatti clans are similar, and intermarriages are common as well. Both clans are governed by a traditional council called *khumbli*, which is in charge of deciding community matters and disputes. The word *Hatti* is probably derived from the word *haat*. The villagers visit the haats, or weekly markets, in the nearby towns to sell their crops.

## SPILLING BLOOD FOR THE SAKE OF PEACE

The annual Jatimara Festival of the Bondas of Odisha is also called Pus Parba. The festival rituals begin in Bonda Hill under Khairput Block in Odisha. The tribal priest sacrifices livestock and birds and offers liquor to the local presiding deities. This is followed by Jhatimara, a decade-old tradition of the Bondas, which is believed to end enmity among the people of the community. This ritual is observed mostly by the males of the Bonda tribe. Bonda youth greet each other and dance to frenzied drumbeats to increase male bonding. Then they stand in pairs and beat each other with sharp tree branches till they draw blood from the wounds inflicted by the blows. As part of the ritual, the priest offers traditional cakes to the youth and urges them to stop fighting. He delivers an effective lecture on friendship and good behaviour. Common sense prevails as the youth embrace each other to become friends for life. Then the Bonda women apply turmeric paste on their wounds, and the universal message of brotherhood and unity is firmly established.

## THE FESTIVAL OF PIG FIGHTS AND CANOE RACES

The Ossuary Festival in the Nicobar Islands is a perfect tribal festival, where the inhabitants of the islands dance to their folk tunes in a circular formation, singing the songs of bravery of their war heroes from ancestry. The locals dress up in traditional attire made of coconut and plantain leaves. Sporting events like pig fights and the canoe race further add to the entertainment value and excitement of the festival.

# 4

# RELIGIOUS RITUALS

Religion is the life of India; religion is the language of this country, the symbol of all its movements.

***– Swami Vivekananda***

## INDIA'S ISRAEL CONNECT

The members of the Bnei Menashe tribe live in Manipur and Mizoram and are descendants of the lost Tribes of Israel. Until the 1960s, they were predominantly Christians. In the seventies these people started to believe that they originally belonged to one of the ten biblical lost tribes of Israel exiled in 722 BC by Assyrian conquerors. They decided to convert back to the religion of their ancestors.

Hence, for more than the past thirty years, the Bnei Menashe people have been practising rituals of Judaism. In 2005, the Bnei Menashe people were acknowledged and accepted as descendants of the tribe of Menashe (Menasseh), the son of Joseph.

## THE ADIS AND THE MISHMIS

Just like the Apatais, two other tribes of Arunachal Pradesh, called the Adi and Mishmi, are followers of an ancient religion known as Donyi Polo, which focuses on nature worship. The meaning of *adi* is 'hill' or 'mountaintop' in their language. The Adi tribe depends on their rice fields, orange orchards and hunting skills to survive.

## GARUDAN THOOKAM – KERALA

In Hindu mythology, the giant eagle Garuda is the king of birds and Lord Vishnu's mount. Garuda helped Goddess Kali in her war campaign against the evil forces by killing the demon Darika. Kerala pays homage to Garuda through a unique and fascinating ritual named Garudan Thookam on Bharani Day in the Kerala calendar months of Kumbham and Makaram. After the conclusion of this dance performance, the backs of the performers impersonating Garuda are pierced with sharp hooks. The dancers then eerily hang from a shaft as they are taken out in this suspended state for a colourful procession to the awe of the spectators.

## AGNI KELI

The Kateel Durga Parameswari Temple in Mangaluru, Karnataka, hosts a seemingly dangerous ritual called Agni Keli in April every year, and it's nothing like April Fool's Day. Hundreds of male devotees stripped to the waist throw burning fronds of palm trees at each other for ritualistic satisfaction. This ancient ritual is part of a festival stretching for eight days, which also features performances based on several themes. As for the burns suffered by the devotees, vermillion powder mixed with water serves to heal the wounds.

## KESH LOCHAN

Mahavira was one of the pioneers of Jainism and hailed from a royal family. When Mahavira became an ascetic, he shed his royal garments. But instead of shaving his head, he plucked out his hair in five handfuls. Today Jains still follow this example. They pluck out each individual strand of hair on their head with their own hands when they renounce worldly attachments. This painful ritual is known as kesh lochan. It is followed because hair is considered a symbol of attachment and pride. The resulting wounds on the head are healed by the application of ash or cow dung.

> Jainism is the sixth-largest religion in India. The majority of Jains can be found in Maharashtra, Rajasthan, Gujarat, Madhya Pradesh and Karnataka.

## AADI FESTIVAL

A priest holds a devotee's head and another smashes a coconut on it in order to help the devotee break free from the past and surrender to God completely. This ritual is celebrated with gusto in Tamil Nadu in the month of Aadi (July–August). Thousands of devotees throng the Mahalakshmi Temple, Mettu Mahadhanapuram, in Karur, Tamil Nadu, at this time of the year to participate in this ritual.

> During the days of the British Raj, there were plans to lay a railway track right across this holy temple. However, the villagers flatly refused to let this happen. The Brits tried to trick them and told them that they could have the right of way if they could break coconuts on their heads. If they managed to do so, the British promised to shift the railway track elsewhere. The villagers took up the challenge and smashed both the coconuts and British pride. However, the ritual is older than this incident and this is not how the ritual originated.

## AYUDHA PUJA

Now here's an ancient Indian ritual that's inspired even the Indian armed forces with all their modern gadgetry, technology and superior fighting methods. Ayudha Puja worships tools and machinery and is integrated within Navratri, celebrated across India. However, the rituals of Navratri differ from state to state. Ayudha Puja is performed in the south Indian states of Karnataka, Tamil Nadu, Andhra Pradesh and Kerala. Weapons, implements, tools and gadgets are worshipped. The deities worshipped along with tools and weapons are Goddess Parvati, the divine mother, Goddess Saraswati, the goddess of wisdom, arts and literature, and Goddess Lakshmi, the goddess of wealth. Today typewriters, computers and printers are also worshipped. The most popular legend behind this festival is that on the day of the festival, Arjuna, the third Pandava, retrieved his weapons from a hole in a tree, where they had been hidden during the exile of the Pandavas. This day is therefore considered auspicious to worship tools and weapons. The battalions of the Indian armed forces perform Ayudha Puja to specifically worship their weapons wherever they are posted.

## THE SHAMANS OF SIKKIM

The spiritual leaders in animist communities are termed as shamans. Shamans are believed to be capable of entering altered states of consciousness, thus communicating supernaturally with trees, animals and spirits of both humans and animals.

> Animism is the belief that plants, objects and natural things have a living soul.

The 1970s witnessed the spread of Buddhism in the region of Dzongu, reserved for the closed community of the Lepchas, who had managed to keep external influences at bay until a few decades ago. Most Lepchas in Dzongu follow the Nyingmapa sect of Buddhism. However, they still retain their animist traditions. So the Buddhist shamans of Dzongu engage in nature worship rituals.

There are 108 clans among the Lepchas, and each clan has a shaman. In the event of a birth, death, wedding, housewarming ceremony, or puja in the family, the shaman is designated to perform the rituals. However, modern times have seen many of the young Lepcha generation migrate out of Dzongu. This has derailed the job responsibilities of the shaman somewhat.

The lives of the Lepchas are synonymous with nature, and Lepcha culture is abundant with stories of the same.

The Lepchas believe that they were moulded out of the snow of the Kanchenjunga Mountain. The original name of Sikkim is *Mayal Lyang*, which means 'secret paradise'. This secret paradise is believed to still exist at the base of the Kanchenjunga. That's why the Lepchas consider the Kanchenjunga as a sacred place. A cloudless and clear sighting of the mountain peak early in the morning is considered auspicious.

After the death of a Lepcha, the shaman guides the souls to a secret paradise. The onset of seasons is heralded by magical birds, which supposedly fly out of the base of the sacred mountain. The birds are a flying weather report about seasonal and weather changes. The racket-tailed drongo is the most important bird in Lepcha culture. The detached racket-shaped feather of this bird is considered a lucky charm, and Lepcha men's traditional hats feature it as an adornment.

Before crossing a river, stream or sacred grove, the shaman makes an offering of flowers, fruit and the local brew named *chi* to the spirits of the forest and seeks their permission to enter the forest.

Chi is the popular local beer brewed from millet and is a key part of all Lepcha activities, be it religious or entertainment. The Lepchas consume generous amounts of chi and also offer it to the gods and spirits on weddings, funerals, house warmings or casual get-togethers. For the Lepchas, anytime is chi time! Another important ritual in January is the worship of the sacred mountain, the Kanchenjunga. An altar is made of wood and flowers, which faces the mountain. An offering of fruit, meat, eggs and chi, of course, is made. The shaman initiates the ritual by requesting the sacred Kanchenjunga to protect her children from harm and calamities and prays for a good harvest. After the ritual is complete, the shaman breaks open three eggs. He turns soothsayer to read the patterns of the broken eggs that form to predict what lies in store for the Lepchas in the near future.

## THE JUGGERNAUT OF THE JAGANNATH RATHAYATRA: THE CHARIOT FESTIVAL

Processions are a must in many major Indian festivals. The Jagannath Rathayatra in Puri is massive in scale. Thousands of people gather in the procession in the Indian state of Odisha. Things can go terribly wrong if any one single event in the planning and organization goes wrong. Three large, richly decorated chariots that resemble the structure of the Jagannath Temple are pulled across the streets all the way to the main temple as the massive crowd follows with shouts of 'Joy Jagannath', or 'Glory to Jagannath'. The idols of Lord Jagannath, his elder brother, Balarama, and their younger sister, Subhadra, are mounted on the huge chariots, which take several months to construct.

> Every year, fifteen days before the rathayatra, Jagannath is believed to fall sick and recuperate. This is also part of the yearly ritual, when visitors are not allowed to see the idol.

This amazing ritual, which takes place in the rainy season every year, is the oldest procession of its kind across the world. It is mentioned in ancient Hindu scriptures like the Brahma Purana, Padma Purana, Skanda Purana and Kapila Samhita.

The three chariots

## BURNING EFFIGIES OF RAVANA: DUSSEHRA

The festival of Dussehra and the ritual of burning effigies of the ten-headed demon king Ravana take place all across India. The enactment of various scenes of the Ramayana, especially the triumph of good over evil in Lord Rama's army defeating the demon forces of Ravana, is the highlight of this festival. Then effigies of Ravana, his brother, Kumbhakarna, and Ravana's son, Meghnad alias Indrajit, are burned to symbolize the victory of good over evil. Dussehra is celebrated twenty days after Diwali on a full-moon day in the month of Ashwin, according to the Hindu calendar. This falls between September and October. The precise date varies every year.

## HEMIS FESTIVAL: LADAKH

The Hemis Festival is celebrated at the monastery of the same name in Ladakh. One of the characteristics of several rituals in India is the recreation and re-enactment of legends and myths. The Hemis Festival follows on the same lines, but the resident lamas or monks perform the re-enactment by wearing masks to portray the several guardian divinities of the Dugpa order of Buddhism. It is held to commemorate the birth anniversary of Guru Padmasambhava, believed by many to be the incarnation of the Buddha. The lamas re-enact their guru's feats, and the music of drums, long horns and cymbals accompany the scene. The beautiful colours, patterns and designs of the masks transport us back in time. The dances and plays performed have a common theme – the triumph of good over evil. This two-day festival, held in the fifth lunar month of the Year of the Monkey, is two hundred years old. The locals dress up in their best traditional clothes to watch the lamas dance and perform.

Ladakhi monks wearing traditional costume and performing Cham dance at Hemis Monastery in Leh, Ladakh

## SELF-FLAGELLATION: MUHARRAM

The practice of the religious ritual of self-flagellation involves hitting oneself with a whip on the body. This takes place across India during Muharram, the Islamic holy month of remembrance and mourning by Shia Muslims to commemorate the martyrdom of Hussein, the grandson of Prophet Muhammad. The mourning period begins on the first day of the first month of the Islamic calendar. The rituals begin with a ten-day fast and end on the Day of Ashura. A procession is taken out in the streets when the masses participate in self-flagellation by periodically whipping their bodies with chains that have sharp blades attached to them. Soon the bodies of the devotees are soaked in their own blood but surprisingly, they seem to feel no pain in their devoted and ecstatic fervour. States with a sizeable Muslim population practise this ritual, such as Assam, West Bengal, Jammu and Kashmir, Uttar Pradesh, Bihar, Kerala and Maharashtra among others.

At a Muharram rally

## THE DEVOUT SHIVA WORSHIPPERS

The Chenchu tribes of Andhra Pradesh live in the central hilly areas in the dense Nallamala Forest. They are Hindu aboriginals with a strong presence in the Prakasam, Mahboobnagar, Kurnool, Nalgonda and Guntur districts. They are perhaps the only Indian tribals who live fearlessly in the terrain of tigers and wild animals. The Chenchu never cut down forest trees as a rule for fuel and collect only dry wood as they consider themselves one with nature. They worship Hindu gods like Hanuman, Lord Shiva (who they call Lingamayya) and so on.

Chenchu legend states that Lord Mallikarjuna, an incarnation of Lord Shiva, fell in love with a young maiden called Chenchu Lakshmi and married her. The tribe believes that they descended from this divine couple. The Chenchu are mentioned in ancient Hindu holy texts like the Puranas, as well as in temple records and chronicles. The diverse rituals of the Chenchus may vary, from being simple to rigid to being wild, intoxicating or mystical. Their passion for dance and having fun demonstrates their exuberance and contentment with whatever little they possess. The Chenchus also worship dargahs (tombs of Muslim saints).

## THE CHANGPAS OF LADAKH

The Changpas of Ladakh are divided into four tribes and further subdivided into fourteen groups. There are 130 families on an average per group. The four major tribes are the Kharnakpas, the Rupshupas, the Korzokpas and the Anghoams, each wandering in their respective territories without encroachment from the others. The Changpas see themselves as Tibetan Buddhists who have incorporated several styles and forms of Buddhism. Their main rituals include Jyabten (purifying themselves by offering food to Lord Padmasambhava) and Tangpe Chona on the fifteenth day of the first month of the lunar calendar to celebrate the victory of good over evil.

## DEITIES OF THE KOLIS OF NIMAR

The Kolis of Nimar in Madhya Pradesh worship Goddess Bhawani as their main deity. Almost every family has a silver image of the goddess at home. Inchirapur has an important shrine dedicated to the goddess, and tribe members perform the hook-swinging rite here in honour of her. Centuries ago, this ritual used a human being to swing, but this practice has been replaced with a bundle of bamboo covered with cloth, keeping safety in mind. The Son Kolis are fishermen who worship the sea as a deity. Some of them believe that their god, Khandoba, is an incarnation of Lord Shiva.

## THE HINDUS WHO BURY THE DEAD

In 1620, many members of the predominantly Hindu Gowdas of Goa converted to Christianity during the Portuguese rule, thus leading to the splitting into two distinct groups with different belief systems. However, these religious beliefs also overlap sometimes. The Hindu Gowdas, for example, do not cremate their dead, in an unusual departure from the Hindu funeral rituals. Instead, they follow the burial practice of their tribal Christian brothers.

### The Stone Age Lifestyle of Goan Tribes

The four main tribes in Goa are the Gowdas, the Kunbis, the Velips and the Dhangars. These tribes live in small groups in separate villages. It's amazing how unique their lifestyle, customs, rituals, traditions, ceremonies, religious beliefs and superstitions are and how these have remained frozen in time over centuries. They, surprisingly, remain untouched by the various changes in the modern world.

## THE ROYAL DESCENDANTS OF THE MOUNTAIN GOD

The Dongria Kondh tribe that lives in the Niyamgiri Hills of Odisha derives its name from *dongar*, meaning 'hill'. However, the name they have kept for themselves is Jharnia or 'protector of streams'. They call the densely forested hills, with their deep gorges and cascading streams, their home. The Dongria Kondh villages lie scattered throughout these hills, the fertile slopes of which are perfect for them to farm and harvest. They worship the mountain god

The fashionable Dongria sport distinctive jewellery, tattoos and hairstyles. Women wear several earrings and three nose rings, while boys wear two nose rings. Dongria girls wear clips in their hair with rings and beads adorning their necks.

Niyam Raja and the hills he rules over. The 4,000-metre Niyam Dongar, or Mountain of the Law, is particularly revered. They believe that they have the right to cultivate Niyamgiri's slopes and that Niyam Raja has granted them these cultivation rights as they are his royal descendants.

### Sacrifices and Ceremonial Rituals

Sacrifices are traditionally made by the Dongria after the harvest and before the new year's crops are planted. Each village has specific sites for sacrifices and the worship of deities of the hills like the mother goddess Dharni, Niyam Raja and others. Each house has sacred spaces for worship. Animal sacrifice in the form of chickens, goats, pigs and particularly buffalo are a part of the rituals. Interestingly, the Dongria Kondh does not have a political or religious leader. Clans and villages have their own separate leaders and individuals like the *beju* and *bejuni*, male and female priests, who oversee certain ceremonial functions.

## THE ELUSIVE NATURE WORSHIPPERS

Until recently, the Madia tribe was totally isolated from the outside world, having no comprehension of clothing, language, health care, education and the other necessities of civilized life. Now, after establishing contact, they have finally started understanding the customs and ways of people living in developed areas. The tribe members are skilled craftsmen and hunters who use the language Madia to communicate. They neither follow nor believe in the major religions of India but worship the forces of nature and their local deities.

### The Madia Tribe: An Overview

The Madia or Madia Gonds or Maria are endogamous tribes found in the Gadchiroli and Chandrapur districts of Maharashtra. The Government of India has granted them the status of 'Primitive Tribal Group'. The Madias live in the Dandakaranya Forest and are one of the oldest Indian tribes, having existed for centuries. The Madia language has no script and features a limited set of words. Despite being inhabitants of Maharashtra, surprisingly, the Madias have no connection with either Marathi or Hindi.

## THE RITUAL OF AGRICULTURAL WORSHIP

The Bhil tribe, found in Nandurbar District of Maharashtra, has its own traditional way of agricultural worship. They invoke and worship their gods and goddesses when they grow various crops during the farming process. The farming ritual of this traditional worship involves the use of alcohol from the *mahua* tree as a key ingredient, with other ingredients like coconut, paddy, black gram lentil, wheat, sorghum, vermilion, incense stick, oil, kumkum, *palash* leaves and the *madar* flower. These rituals involve three stages. The first stage begins when the farming cycle starts in April, after *Gudi Padava*, the spring festival that also ushers in the Maratha New Year. This is when the new crops are prepared. After the farmers have worshipped the deities, the farming process begins as the fields are prepared. Before the process of tilling the field, a stone is placed at the eastern corner of the field. The ordinary stone is then made sacred. Initially, water is offered to the stone, followed by oil as incense sticks are burned and *kumkum* and vermilion are applied on the stone. The *mahua* liquor is sprinkled on the stone with *palash* leaves and also in centre of the farming field. Rice is kept with the alcohol everywhere as the farmers pay homage to Mother Earth, or *Kani Kansari*, and invoke her to receive her blessings for a bountiful harvest. They pray: *O Mother Earth, O Kani-Kansari, I begin the cultivation process today in your name and pray that the Kani-Kansari should always continue to prosper, therefore I worship you in the name of Kani Mata.*

The second stage of worship takes place during the sowing process. The Bhil pray to their numerous gods and goddesses to protect their crops and grant them a plentiful harvest. In August, no farming work takes place in the fields for five days, which includes two Sundays and three Tuesdays. This is when the Bhils perform their worship rituals. On the first Sunday, they begin by worshipping blue grass and wood. After this, the grass is cut, and the sowing begins. The process of daubing the house takes place only after the grain is fetched.

The second Sunday sees a tiger deity being worshipped as all the male members of the village assemble under a huge *peepal* tree on the outskirts of the village. The actions of a tiger are impersonated by someone, and another man imitates a cat, and everybody chants in unison, 'Here comes the tiger, here comes the tiger, run.'

But in a stark difference between words and action, the makeshift tiger and cat are made to run instead. The villagers pelt them with balls of wet mud. This is basically a ritual of scaring the tiger away from the village. This ritual is the exclusive domain of the males, who also prepare food from the ingredients fetched by all the members from their homes. On the third, fourth and fifth Tuesdays, the Bhil men simply stay at home and relax instead of going to work in the fields.

When the harvesting begins, the granary is cleaned first before anything else, and the threshing floor is prepared.

Before beginning harvesting, the farmers tie turbans on their heads and pour water, oil and vermilion on a stone at the threshing floor as part of a ritual that worships and invokes the gods and goddesses the family favours, like Modi Mata, Kani Mata, Surya Dev (sun god) and Dhatri Mata (Mother Earth). Palash leaves with alcohol are sprinkled on the floor, and rice is kept alongside. The threshing floor is daubed with cow dung first. The next day, this area is worshipped in a ritual with coconut, incense sticks, *kumkum* and rice. Finally, the new crop is fetched for the threshing or cleaning process. After harvesting the crop and bringing it home, the farmers offer a small portion for oblation to their favoured goddess. A bamboo basket, placed on a white dhoti, is packed with ingredients like coconut, mahua alcohol, betel, dried date, all kinds of green vegetables, rice, fenugreek leaves, paddy, sorghum, incense sticks, matchsticks, vermilion, kumkum, oil and eleven rupees among other ingredients. Then the basket is tied with the dhoti and taken to the temple to be offered to favoured goddess like Mogi Mata. At the end of these worship rituals, people return home to their respective families. The family members have a meal together to consume the freshly cooked new grains. Thus ends the third stage.

## THE EYE OF THE TIGER

Between Dusshera and Diwali, when India recuperates from the lengthy period of festivities and gears up to light up their homes, the Korkus, a Munda ethnic group found mainly in Madhya Pradesh and certain parts of Maharashtra, get ready to celebrate their own unique annual ritual. This ritual takes place in the Melghat Tiger Reserve (MTR) and the other forested areas of the Satpura mountain range, the home of these tribals. They walk to the shrines located closest to their hamlet to worship the tiger, whom they consider one of their main protector deities. They pray to the tiger to keep them safe when they graze in the forest and not harm their cattle or livestock. They request the tiger to protect them from the other wild animals that inhabit the forest and to ward off the evil eye. Most tiger shrines are located on the outskirts of villages, right on the edge of the forest. The shrines have only a pair of stones that lie under a large teak tree, which are ensconced by several other trees of teak and palash.

## WORSHIPPERS OF RAVANA

The Korkus consider Mahadev or Lord Shiva as the father of the gods. On Shivaratri, the Korkus offer water, flowers and fruits to Lord Shiva. They also worship Ravana as a god, in the belief that Ravana's severe penance to Lord Shiva gave birth to the Korkus. Meghnad, the son of Ravana, is also worshipped by the Korkus during Dussehra. They believe that Meghnad saved them during wars. Hence, every village must have a pole to worship Meghnad. The Meghnad pole can be short or long. Though the Korku language is termed as one of the 196 endangered languages by UNESCO, there are still some groups like the Potharia Korku who have preserved the language. The Potharia Korku group lives somewhere in the Vindhya Mountains.

Korku women performing folk dance

## THE THARUS

The Tharu people of Uttar Pradesh are certainly a multi-talented community, dabbling in various survival modes like cultivation, animal rearing, fishing, professional hawking, basketry, masonry and carpentry. But this tribe has an unusual religious ritual of animal sacrifice and human body sacrifice. The Tharus are a multicultural community and a religious melting pot, who follow Hinduism, Islam, Buddhism, Christianity and animism. However, the intricate religious rituals focus on deity worship, irrespective of the religion followed by any particular family. The objective of animal ritual sacrifices is to appease deities in the event of natural calamities or when the Tharus wish to prevent diseases. Special rituals are linked with these sacrifices of chickens, pigeons and other animals given in offerings to god along with milk and gorgeous silk clothes. The job of pleasing gods to cure diseases and defeating evil forces is given to Tharu doctors called shamans, who beat their drums loudly and offer these sacrifices.

## THE MEDICINE MAN OF THE DHARUA

The Dharua of Odisha mix their religious rituals of animism with certain elements of Hinduism. They think that animals, birds and trees possess souls just like humans. The Dharua pray to the spirit in charge of rain and river water and ask to be blessed with good catches of fish and abundant crops. They are scared of the spirit Rau, who brings down his victims by shooting small stone or clay pieces at their backs. Only a medicine man can extract these small pieces of stone, which can cause death otherwise. These small stone pieces are surprisingly invisible to the human eye, except the eyes of the medicine man, of course.

### The Three Worlds

The Dharuas believe in the existence of three worlds. The earth is considered the 'middle' world, the home of human beings and supernatural creatures. The sky, or the 'upper' world, is where the supreme spirit, or the 'high god' can be found, who is believed to be the creator and considered supreme to all other gods. The third world is the 'underworld', or the abode of the dead.

## THE RONG CURSE

The Lepchas of Dzongu call themselves 'Rong' or 'ravine dwellers'. Originally, the Lepchas were nomadic hunters who foraged for food. Later, they started shifting cultivation, armed with primitive technology. The Lepchas follow animism, worshipping the natural spirits of their surrounding land, water and trees. Lepcha clans also worship particular mountain peaks as their guardian deities, claiming a mythical connection with these mountains, like Simvo, Siniolchu and Kanchenjunga, which are an integral part of Lepcha culture and folklore. The Lepchas have been worshipping the Kanchenjunga Mountain for centuries.

They feel the mountain is the protector of all creatures, and everything associated with the mountain is perceived as sacred by them. Lepcha folklore declares that Dzongu is the bridge to Mayal Lyang, a heavenly abode hidden in a distant, secret location. The Mayal Lyang is believed to be the origin of the Lepchas and their eventual destination after death to lead a peaceful afterlife. Mayal Lyang means the 'Hidden Land' or 'Land blessed by God' in Lepcha parlance. In an interesting ancient Lepcha folk tale, the Lepchas had cast curses across the Dzongu Valley. Some of the Bhutia ancestors could not pay for the cattle they had taken from their Lepcha neighbours. This is why Lepcha shamans of Dzongu sent these curses towards the Bhutias. These shamans are called Bongthing outside of Dzongu but are known as Padims within the reserve area. The Bhutias residing in the area still perform annual rituals to counter the curse of the Lepcha shamans so that their cultivations remain unaffected. There's a price to pay for unpaid cattle!

### The Forbidden Dzongu Valley

The Dzongu region looks straight out of a fairy tale at first sight, made up of thirty-odd sparsely populated mountain villages nestled cosily among deep gorges, lush, forested hills and gorgeous valleys. Located in the foothills of the world's third highest mountain, Kanchenjunga, it is the last frontier of land before the mighty Himalayas begin its impressive stretch. Dzongu is the glorious centre that brings out of the best of Sikkim's culture. Not only is it among the most culturally rich places of Sikkim but one that still has its local traditions and vibrant culture intact.

The mixing of cultures and the arrival of the Nepalese in droves later led to the erosion of the original traditions and beliefs. Dzongu was therefore declared a special reserve area for the Lepchas in the early sixties by the Chogyals of the Sikkim Kingdom. The objective was to preserve the social homogeneity of the tribe, and it became the exclusive home of only 'pure-blooded' Lepchas.

## THE SANTHAL RELIGIOUS PRACTITIONERS

The Santhals have a staggering 150 spirit deities, generally called *bongas*. Each village has a sacred grove, where we find these bongas. These deities are generally benevolent, the sole exception being the forest bongas, who are malevolent, being the souls of people who died unnatural deaths. The village priest, or *naeke*, and his wife represent the original Santhal couple. The naeke's functions are limited to only festivals and annual ceremonies. He makes the animals sacred before they are offered to the grove deities. On the other hand, the Santhal *ojha*, who is the healer and diviner, has more power and several functions. He chases away the malevolent deities, deduces the causes of disease and cures them. His vast medicinal knowledge comes from the basic magical formulas or mantras inherited from his master, but he also innovates using his own experience. He also sacrifices his own blood to the bongas sometimes for which he charges a fee.

## THE GHOSTS OF THE BONDAS

Despite being animistic, the Bondas also worship Hindu gods. However, they consume beef and the meat of dead animals. The Bondas link themselves with Lord Rama and his sword named *patkhanda*. This sword of Rama is believed to be located in a great banyan tree. Mahaprabhu is their supreme deity. The Bondas also worship the sun and the moon and several demigods that the believe live in streams, forests, swiddens, villages and homes. These demigods can be good or evil and are worshipped in different shrines. But this worship usually takes place at the *sindibor*, which is a sacred stone platform constructed in each village, where important socio-religious activities are also conducted. The *disharie*s, or shamans, act as go-betweens among these supernatural powers and the Bondas. The Bondas consider malevolent entities as the ones who have died recently. The wrath of these ghosts is thought to lead to crop failures, the death of domestic animals and diseases. Fearing these ghosts, the Bondas

A Bonda woman in traditional attire

refuse to venture out alone at night. If needed, they go out in groups and sing songs loudly to keep away these evil, ghostly spirits.

### The Most Famous Bonda

Dambaru Sisa created history when he became the first MLA (member of the Legislative Assembly) in India from the Bonda tribe, to which he traces his ancestry. Dambaru Sisa's main aim is to protect the traditions and culture of the Bonda people and to provide them with educational opportunities.

At a Bonda haat (market)

# 5

# FOOD AND DRINK RITUALS

The growing issue of food waste is a concern as there are millions who go without food every day.

***– Sachin Tendulkar***

## THE SINGPHOS: INDIA'S FIRST TEA DRINKERS?

The Buddhist tribe of the Singphos is considered one of the first tea drinkers of India. Their process of making tea is certainly unique as they first heat the tea leaves in a metal pan till the leaves turn brown. Then the tea leaves are sun-dried for a few days before consumption. Next time you are in Arunachal Pradesh, remember to sip some Singpho tea!

## CULTURAL AND RITUALISTIC SIGNIFICANCE OF TRIBAL CUISINE

Food plays a key role during tribal rituals, ceremonies, and festivals in India. For example, the Baiga Festival that takes place in Madhya Pradesh witnesses special millets and meat dishes that are specially made and served to local deities. Also, food and nature are synonymous, forging a unique relationship that sees the use of medicinal herbs, consumption of wild greens and sustainable hunting practices by the tribe's hunters for food. All the Indian tribes have an arsenal of ecological knowledge, and they dip into its reserves constantly for food, as well as their survival, by co-existing with nature. The figure is especially staggering when one considers that Indian communities consume an estimated 6,000 varieties of rice, over 500 types of millets and hundreds of herbs and vegetables. Even with a country as diverse as India, the sheer variety on offer is mind-boggling, to say the least. This diverse and rich range of cooking is also enhanced by the ever-evolving fusion of food between two regions and the evolving cooking techniques of both traditional and modern India. Consider the fact that Indians were consuming stems, stalks and vegetable peels much before the world realized the advantages of zero-waste cooking.

## CULTURAL AND RITUALISTIC SIGNIFICANCE OF THE COCONUT

The coconut is conspicuous by its presence in all rituals, ceremonies and festivals and also in several dishes across India. It finds a place in post-Vedic works, such as the famous epics, the Ramayana and the Mahabharata, the Puranas and the Jataka stories of Buddhism. In fact, there is an interesting account in Hindu mythology about the birth of the coconut. It is believed that baby Ganesha wanted a toy to play with and was given a coconut by Lord Shiva. That's how the much-loved coconut was supposedly born, and that's why the coconut is important while worshipping Lord Ganesha.

> The coconut is called *narikela* in Sanskrit. *Niyor* means 'oil' and *kolai* means 'nut', which are derived from two words of South Asian origin. The coconut is also referred as *sriphala*, or 'the god's fruit', in Sanskrit. This denotes its importance from ancient times.

The coconut is presented to guests during marriages, religious festivals and other ritualistic ceremonies. Historians have revealed it was an integral part of the religious rites of the Agni Purana and the Brahma Purana dating back to 800–900 CE. In fact, priests in south India reportedly do not accept a devotee's offerings if the coconut is missing.

The coconut is also considered to possess medicinal uses. Hindus believe that planting a coconut tree in the garden of a house fetches prosperity. The coconut symbolizes fertility. During wedding rituals, the coconut is placed in a pot, which symbolizes the womb. The coconut, being a symbol of life, is supposed to grant the gift of fertility to the couple. Because of this, women who are pregnant are not supposed to break the coconut as this is like taking a life. The belief that the sound of the breaking coconut harms the foetus in the womb is also responsible for pregnant women being discouraged from smashing open coconuts. However, the breaking of a coconut also signifies the breaking of one's *ahankara*, or ego. The coconut is a symbol of a noble and proud heart that has a tough exterior shell and sweet, delicate fruit within. The fleshy, white portion of the coconut is considered to represent the brain, which is self-centred, egotistical and jealous.

During traditional Gujarati wedding rituals, the bride gifts the groom a coconut during their wedding, and the husband is supposed to preserve this coconut for the rest of his life. Now, that's a tough nut to crack. The Kunbis hailing from the Konkan region of Maharashtra also believe in preserving the coconut in memory of their ancestors.

The coconut is everywhere in India, just like a superhero. It finds a place in the marriage proposal, it is used as a symbol of betrothal, used to welcome the bride to her new home and protects against the evil eye. Tribes like the Gond and the Bhil in Rajasthan, Gujarat and Madhya Pradesh use the coconut for their marriage rituals and death rites.

The Assamese celebrate their Magh Bihu Festival with great pomp and gusto in January. They prepare delicious coconut sweet dishes like *laru* and *narikol pitha*. During the harvest festival after the conclusion of the harvesting season, the coconut is a star in all rural Indian households.

Aadi Perukku is celebrated in Tamil Nadu for the life-giving properties and sustainability of water. The rituals involve the devotees breaking coconuts on their heads.

In Kerala, fishermen place a coconut in the turbulent sea to calm it down before they go fishing in the hope of a good catch. In Daman and Diu on the west coast and in the coastal regions of Maharashtra, like Thane, Konkan and Ratnagiri, Narali Purnima is observed. This festival celebrates the beginning of the fishing season and the water trade. Fishermen offer prayers to Lord Varuna, the sea god, for an abundant catch in his waters, a smooth fishing journey and a profitable business. Celebrations include singing and dancing, as well as feasting on the traditional and delicious cuisine of sweet coconut rice and fish curry.

## THE RITUAL OF OFFERING BHOG TO THE GODS

Most of the Hindu communities and tribes in India participate in a small ritual when they are worshipping God. They offer *bhog*, or *naivedyam*, to the deity, which is later distributed to everyone who participates in the ritual and worship as *prasad*. This bhog is usually *saatvic* in nature and often consists of sweets. Bhogs can be cooked food too.

Many devotees feel that they should offer God what they eat themselves. Hence, there are Indian deities who also 'consume' meat, fish and liquor, which they receive as offerings. Even the Vedas recommend a choice of 50 animals from a list of 250 that are suitable to be sacrificed to the gods. Here are some unusual offerings that a select few offer to their deities.

- Goddess Kali is often offered animals as sacrifice along with blood to quench her thirst. The goat is the common choice in West Bengal. However, the Chinese community of Kolkata prefers to serve dumplings, fried rice and chopsuey to the goddess at their Kali temple.
- Deities like Kali and Kaal Bhairav are often offered alcohol as bhog. This ritual of offering liquor is symbolic of devotion and surrender.
- A suburb in Surat named Katargram offers cigarettes as offerings in the shrine that is dedicated to Mamadev Baba. Live life kingsize!
- In Alibaug, a coastal town of Maharashtra, locals love their fish and meat. On the first day of Ganesh Chaturthi, devotees offer a huge non-vegetarian spread to Lord Ganesha to welcome him that comprises prawns, dried shrimp, crabs, chicken and mutton.
- The Tantric deities are given offerings of the pleasure of the five senses by their devotees. A *kapala*, or cup made of skull, has either red wine signifying blood or unbaked dough cakes that are made from butter and barley flour. These cakes are realistically made and coloured in the shape of human organs like the nose, tongue, eyes, ears and heart.

## THE BUDGET HALWA RITUAL

The Halwa ritual is an interesting customary ceremony observed in the final stage of the preparation of the Union Budget. It is performed every year before the lock-in process of the Union Budget. The passion that Indians have for food and their sweet tooth is prominently displayed in this ritual as an Indian sweet dish called the *halwa* is prepared in a large container called the *kadhai* at the North Block. The finance minister stirs the kadhai in a symbolic gesture and serves the halwa to all the officials and staff involved in the process of making the budget. After the conclusion of the halwa ritual, the budget documents are printed in the basement of the North Block before being presented in the Indian Parliament. The Halwa ritual also marks the beginning of the lockdown of the finance ministry as no official is allowed to leave the ministry compound till the budget is presented in Parliament. Well, if the budget isn't sweet, the Halwa surely is! Bon appétit!

# 6

# SOCIAL RITUALS

Unlike a drop of water which loses its identity when it joins the ocean, man does not lose his being in the society in which he lives.

**– *Bhim Rao Ambedkar***

## THE UNIQUE NYISHI HOUSEWARMING CEREMONY

During a Nyishi housewarming ceremony, guests and hosts play a giant game called adi *eggtung*, which involves friendly arguments and teasing each other. They also share stories about the house and challenge each other with riddles. The storytelling at these housewarming sessions involves tales passed down orally through generations. There is a strong community bond as elders and youngsters all gather for these celebrations. The Nyishi home is definitely where the heart is!

## THE CHILDREN OF THE BIG RIVER

The word *dimasa* in Assamese means 'children of the big river'. The Dimasa property is divided into three parts – paternal, maternal and common. The son inherits the paternal property, which consists of cash money, cattle and land. The daughter gets the maternal property, which is made up of all the jewellery, clothes and accessories. The common property means the family utensils and household equipment, which is shared by the son and the daughter. The Dimasa are patriarchal in terms of family structure. However, both the patrilineal and matrilineal systems co-exist peacefully within Dimasa society, making it a bi-lineal type of society. This unique feature is absent in all other tribes of north-east India. Each man and woman in the Dimasa tribe belongs to two clans. A boy and a girl inherit the patriclan and matriclan of their father and mother. Also, a father and a son belong to the same patriclan, but they have two different matriclans. The father inherits his matriclan from his maternal grandmother, while the son does so from his own maternal grandmother. If that's not confusing enough, consider that the patriclan of a woman changes immediately after her marriage when she is given the husband's patriclan through a ceremony called the *Khelrabriba* or *Madaikhilimba*. However, her matriclan remains unchanged. It is said that these clans were created by King Krishna Chandra Narayan around 1800 CE. The king initially created seven *sengphongs* and seven *julus*. Little did he know that they would increase to forty and forty-two respectively over the years. More about this clan has been discussed in the first chapter.

## THE AMAZING FESTIVAL OF THE ANGAMI NAGAS

The Angamis celebrate a festival called Sekrenyi (sometimes also called Phousanyi) for as long as ten days in February. *Sekrenyi* is a sanctification festival (*sekre* = sanctification; *nyi* = feast; *thenyi* = festival). The festival is held after the harvest season and features a series of rituals. The first is the *kizie*, when a few drops of rice water from a jug named *zumho* are applied to leaves. The lady of the household then places these at the three main posts of the house. On the first day, everyone goes to the village well to bathe. The previous night, the well is cleaned and guarded by the village youth, and no one is allowed to fetch water from the well after it is cleaned, especially women. The next morning, the young men of the village wake up early to attend the washing ritual at the well. Wearing two new shawls, called the white *mhoushü* and the black *lohe*, they sprinkle water on their chests, knees and right arms. This ritual is called *dzüseva*, or 'touching the sleeping water'. They believe the well water washes away all misfortunes from their lives. After they return from the well, a rooster is sacrificed. It's considered a good omen if the right leg of the rooster falls over the left leg as it falls.

The fourth day of the festival features singing and feasting that continues for three days. The *thekra hie* is another ritual when the young people of the village sit together to sing traditional songs all day, with jugs of rice beer and plates of meat provided to them. On the seventh day, it is hunting time for the young men. The most important ceremony is held on the eighth day when the bridge-pulling or gate-pulling happens and inter-village visits happen. All field work comes to a standstill during this festival of songs and feasting.

## DRESSING STYLE OF MIZO WOMEN

- Mizo women wear the puanchei on weddings and other special occasions. This is a traditional two-piece outfit with something similar to a long skirt worn below and a top or shirt worn above. This comes in varieties known as *chapchar kut*, *mim* kut and *pawl* kut. These two pieces are brightly coloured, featuring checkered designs.
- The women sport a headdress when they dance. It is made of brass and coloured cane. Porcupines decorate these headgears, and the upper edges are enhanced by green parrot feathers.
- They wear attractive blouses called *kawrchei* and *ngotekherh* above the puanchei during their dances. Kawrchei is made of cotton and is normally handwoven. *Zakuolaisen* is a beautiful blouse with crimson stripes worn by unmarried females, while the married ones wear *puon pie*.

## WORSHIPPING SPIRITS

The Birhor tribes of Jharkhand perform various ceremonies to appease the spirits and seek their protection and blessings. They believe that their ancestors are still present in the form of spirits and can influence their lives. They worship and seek guidance from their ancestors through rituals, prayers and offerings.

## THE STRANGE BURIAL GROUND

Some Birhor communities do not have proper burial grounds. They cannot afford to buy land for their graveyards, and hence, they are looking for help from the district government. These Birhors are in forest communities like Tatiba, Kundrugutu and Kayra located in West Singbhum District of Jharkhand. They are a small percentage of the state's tribal population – 0.06 per cent of the total 8.6 million tribals in Jharkhand. They bury the dead wherever they find a little vacant land available. The funeral customs of the Birhor have existed for a hundred years. The main reason for conducting the funeral ceremony was to prevent any harm from coming to their *tanda*, or temporary settlement, from the spirit of the dead. However, it was also performed to protect the spirit of the recently deceased from being harmed by stray spirits.

The body is prepared by being washed first and then smeared with oil and turmeric. If the deceased was married, a vermilion mark is applied on the forehead. The body is then placed on a stretcher and carried headfirst by the Birhor men and taken to the cremation ground or burial ground. Spirits are thought to be harmful for men if women and children die within twenty-one days of childbirth. To protect the man from harm, the women become pallbearers. A *mati*, or spirit doctor, enters a state of possession and communicates with the dangerous spirit. The mati informs the spirit of a hill or forest that he is handing over the spirit of the deceased to him to guard and ensure that it remains there without returning to the village. Once the burial ground on the outskirts of the village is reached, the corpse is placed on the ground for some time. Then it is taken to the open grave and carried three times around it before being placed in it with the head pointing southwards. If the body has to be cremated, the son or grandson of the deceased is the one who lights the funeral pyre.

## MUNDA BIRTH RITUALS

After a Munda woman is discovered to be pregnant, the Mundas offer sacrifices to their deity, Garasibonga. The other birth rituals of the Munda tribe include the Chhathi ritual, which takes place three, six or nine days after childbirth. This is done to disinfect the infant. The child's hair is shaved, and later, the child is thrown into the pond as the first swimming lesson. No wonder the Mundas are excellent swimmers. The guests and relatives then shower blessings on the baby.

Group photo of Mundas – Chota Nagpur, 1903

- **The Naming Ceremony:** The day after the Chhathi ritual is celebrated as the naming ceremony of the child. During this, rice grains are dropped in water as various names are pronounced. If the grains coincide, then that name is selected as the child's name. If it does not match, the process continues till the desired result is achieved.
- ***Sutam Tol:*** On the next day, a black thread is tied around the waist of the newborn child to ward off the evil eye. This protective ritual is called Sutam Tol.
- **Ear Boring Ceremony:** This ritual takes place during the first three years of the child in a winter month. Barbers are summoned, who smear the lobule of the child's ear with vermillion, using a silver or copper

ear borer. This is followed by the sacrifice of a fowl or goat and blessings bestowed on the child by the invited guests.

## MUNDA DEATH RITUALS

The Mundas believe that after a person dies, their spirit roams about the remains of the body. It can only find its permanent resting place provided certain rites are observed. The relatives of the deceased shave their hair and bathe to purify themselves between the third and fifth day after the person has passed away. Saplings of the *tiril* tree are planted and placed carefully in an earthen vessel. The spirit of the dead is summoned by shouting out his name. Later, prayers are offered, and rituals are carried out in his name for the soul's peace in the afterlife.

### The Munda Tribe: An Overview

The Munda tribe can be found in over four Indian states. Although they are mainly concentrated in Jharkhand, they are present in neighbouring states like West Bengal, Bihar, Odisha and Chhattisgarh. Currently, roughly two million Mundas reside in India. This tribal community is one of the oldest in South Asia. However, this tribe got the respect it deserved between 1857 and 1928 because of a man named Birsa Munda.

Birsa Munda was considered a prophet by his tribe. His godlike status is evident among the tribals as he is referred to by many as Bhagawan Birsa Munda. He was one of the major leaders who led the movement against British colonial rule in the tribal belt of Bihar and Jharkhand. He was captured by the British at the age of twenty-five, and he breathed his last in Ranchi Jail in 1900. Honoured by the Government of India, Birsa Munda is the sole tribal leader whose portrait hangs proudly in the Central Hall of the Indian Parliament.

## THE SEXUALLY LIBERATED MURIAS

It is often believed that every act of the Muria is focused on the realization of sex. However, such progressive sexual realization, where a regular switching of sexual partners is encouraged, demands strict rules that are not always easy to follow. Muria law states that no boy (*chelik*) or girl (*motiari*) may sleep with the same person more than three times in a row. This is to do away with preferential treatment. Sex education is an important part of the curriculum, and children are taught sexual techniques by their elders through actual instruction.

## THE TRIBE WITH THE BEST SEXUAL COMPATIBILITY

The Bison-Horn Maria people encourage premarital sex to ensure sexual compatibility between romantic partners before marriage so that they can be wedded happily ever after. The most admirable thing, however, is that if children are born as a result of premarital sex between two partners, they are granted the same respect and rights as children born out of legal marriages.

## KORKU DEATH RITUALS

The Korkus believe that everyone should die on the floor as everyone is born on earth. If a Korku dies on a bed, it is no longer used as the family members are scared that the dead person's spirit might linger on the bed and harm others using it. The Korkus undress the dead body, which is then wrapped up with a white loincloth. When a married woman dies, a red cloth is used instead of white. The dead body is buried in the graveyard, with the head facing south. Before the body is buried, a pot that has rice water is broken near the head of the corpse. Bread pieces, egg, turmeric, milk, wine, *kutki* (also called little millet), *khichdi* and tobacco are thrown inside the grave before burial to ensure the peace of the soul in the afterlife. Then the nearest relative, be the husband or the son, throws earth into the grave, which is filled up by the rest of the family members. A memorial post called *mando* is created using wood and stones to remember the deceased. Below this memorial post, there's a human figure with arms wide open and the figure of a horse rider to denote that their ancestor is on his way to heaven because of their good deeds. Images of the sun and moon are also erected on these figures because they believe that the dead Korku will go to the sun, which is heaven, through the moon. The final nail in the coffin is a sumptuous feast called *sidoli*, after which the spirit finally rests. All the villagers and relatives engage in singing, dancing and the consumption of local liquor called sidu. When nothing is constant in life, sidu is, even after death. In the evening, a lavish feast is arranged. The old women sing the same songs during this feast that they had sung earlier at the funeral function.

## MORE KORKU SOCIETY RITUALS

- The Korkus have several methods to bring about early delivery in a pregnant woman. A twisted thread is untwined before her eyes, or she is given water to drink in which her husband's left leg, a gun barrel, a pestle or a thunderbolt have been washed. To ensure a smooth delivery, a pregnant woman is made to lie down and drink the water with which her husband's leg is washed. They feed the pregnant woman the tongue of a tiger so that the baby born is brave. The Korku also have methods to try and make a barren woman give birth. She is given a strand of hair from the head of a woman who has successfully given birth to many children and asked to bury the strand below her bathing stone. This hair transplant supposedly transfers the lucky woman's fertility to the barren woman.
- The Korkus do not eat anything before they go hunting as they believe that god might send game their way if he sees they are hungry. The Korku hunter also does not sleep with his wife the night before the hunt.

- Another strange Korku belief is that naked women driving a plough will bring about good rainfall.
- The Korku are fond of getting tattoos done on their body, except for their legs. They think that nothing will go with them to God's abode after their death except these tattoos. Tattooing is also supposed to make their dead ancestors happy.

## THE BISHNOIS

The Bishnoi sect was formed by Guru Jambheshwar after there was a severe drought in the Marwar region of Rajasthan. The Guru created a community with twenty-nine principles or doctrines that were to be followed. The name Bishnoi is derived from these twenty-nine doctrines as *bishnoi* means 'twenty-nine' in the local dialect. These doctrines are composed of twenty Hindu and nine Muslim principles with respect for nature as the main objective. Ten doctrines stress personal hygiene and the maintenance of good basic health, seven doctrines emphasize healthy social behaviour, and five urge them to worship God. Eight doctrines advise on the preservation of biodiversity and encourage good animal husbandry.

Guru Jambheshwar directed the worship of Lord Vishnu and banned the killing of animals, as well as the cutting down of trees. The Bishnois are strictly vegetarian and passionate protectors of trees and wildlife. In 1730 CE, the king of Jodhpur sent his army to cut down trees to create space for his new palace to be built. The Bishnoi people hugged the trees to prevent them from being cut down and shielded them using their bodies. After axing 363 people, common sense prevailed as the king declared the Khejarli region a preserve. This event inspired the famous Chipko movement in the 1970s in Uttarakhand (then part of Uttar Pradesh).

Bishnoi women

## WOMEN EMPOWERMENT AMONG THE GOWDAS

The tribal community of the Gowdas is considered to be the first settlers in Goa. However, no written documentation exists to prove this fact about their origins, although they have been linked to the Gowda community from Bengal, which has similar customs and rituals. Historians believe they have taken their name from the word *gaon*, meaning 'village' in Sanskrit. Gowdas practise Hinduism but lack a hierarchical order, unlike other Hindu tribes. They prefer not to marry outside their own community and also allow cross-cousin marriages between paternal and maternal cousins. Women play important roles in economic, social and political activities, but strangely, are not allowed to participate in any religious rituals, not even the rites associated with the deity that is worshipped in the house. The tribe worships Lord Mallikarjuna, an avatar of Lord Shiva. Despite the exclusion from religious affairs, which is strictly a male domain, Gowda women have been bestowed a diverse range of rights in the economic, social, and political spheres. Widows solely inherit their husbands' property after their deaths, a tradition glaringly absent in most other Indian tribes.

## THE WEEPING KOKNAS

Many of us weep after the death of a loved one. But for the Koknas of Maharashtra, this is a compulsory death ritual. The family members weep loudly, lamenting the death of their loved one. The villagers are informed about the death with loud drumbeats. Death is known as *maiyat* among the Koknas. In their death ritual, the dead body is laid on a stone grinder. If it's a man, his body is covered by a white cloth, and in the case of a woman, a red cloth is used to cover the corpse. The dead body is then dressed in new clothes and adorned with flowers, rice and money. Weapons like the axe and *dhariya*, a sharp instrument used for cutting, are kept with the dead body of a man so that the witches don't harass or trouble him. The son lights the firewood heap after the dead body is placed over it. After the completion of this ritual, the family members have a bath as a cleansing ritual and go home. The custom of *barma* involves feeding the relatives on the twelfth day after death. However, many Koknas offer *shraddha* like the Hindus these days.

The Kokna people

## THE CHILD-NAMING CEREMONY

On the fifth day of delivery, the Koknas have the *panchuro* function, where a few women from the neighbourhood are invited along with relatives by family members. The child is given a bath and moves from hand to hand. A *dai* and other women ring a plate loudly and give the child advice for life, like being obedient, brave and clever. The child is then handed back to the mother. The name of the child is given by the father's sister. Modern Kokna parents, however, name their child based on the zodiac sign as given by a brahmin.

### THE KOKNAS: A BRIEF OVERVIEW

The Kokna tribe is found in a few districts of Maharashtra, but they have a sizeable presence in Gujarat, residing in the Valsad, Ahwa-Dang and Navsari districts. They are also found in states like Karnataka, Rajasthan and the Union Territory of Dadra and Nagar Haveli. They speak the Indo-Aryan language but can also speak and read Marathi, Devanagari and Hindi. Anthropologists believe that the ancestors of the Kokna were the primary inhabitants of the Konkan region, and that the present-day Konkani language evolved from their ancient dialects.

## BONDA DEATH RITES

After death or *mora*, a Bonda is cremated on a funeral pyre, but the cause of death is also determined in a unique post-mortem. The surviving spouse visits the cremation ground, takes a piece of half-burnt bone and strikes it with a pebble. If the bone crumbles, the death is not due to sorcery. If it doesn't crumble, the culprit is identified by a shaman using his magical method. When the guilty party is identified, he is penalized by the village, or revenge is taken with the help of magical practices. When death or mora takes place, Bonda custom demands that a cow be sacrificed on the tenth day. This practice is known as *gaitang*. This is followed by a feast, which is held for the kin and 'Soru-brothers', basically a socio-religious

Bonda brotherhood group. If the descendant is incapable financially, he is granted time up to twelve months to feed the Soru-brothers. Otherwise, he has the option of taking a loan from any fellow villager for the feast and becomes his bonded labour. The Soru-brothers must be fed at any cost.

### Bonda Women Empowerment

Women are granted a privileged position in Bonda society. They are the main workers and food providers for the Bondas. This matriarchal dominance exists in the marriage system, too, as Bonda women tend to marry boys who are at least five to ten years younger. The wife takes care of her husband as he grows up to be a man, and he takes care of his older wife, in turn, later in life. The women are artistically inclined, making Worli paintings in their homes. In sharp contrast with most of India, the number of Bonda women far outnumbers the number of men. The Bondas receive training in arms at a young age. They still use the *binnimaya pratha*, or barter system, customarily visiting a market every Sunday.

## SANTHAL DEATH RITUALS

Santhals believe that their souls become bongas three generations after death, that is if all the rituals have been performed to perfection. At cremation, the chief mourner, usually the eldest son, collects a few bones, which are kept for some time under the rafters of the house. These bones are then washed and offered milk, rice beer and sacred water by the female mourners of the family. This mourning ritual reflects the central Santhal symbolism of flower and bone, which complement each other. The feeding of bones crowned by flowers symbolizes the principle of descent, represented by the bone, and is also symbolic of the principle of affinity as the flower represents the uterus. During this ritual, the chief mourner is possessed by a spirit and starts behaving like it. He is then questioned by the village priest, and this dialogue certifies that the spirit has reached the other world. A year later, the bones are immersed in water, a ritual that also involves a goat sacrifice. The dead now becomes an ancestor who's still known by his name. A month later, a ritual text releases him from his identity, and he becomes a nameless ancestor. He now joins the other ancestors in the ancestral room of the house to whom rice beer is offered along with the others. His shadow, which was earlier roaming between the two worlds, now goes to Hanapuri, the abode of the dead, which is ruled by Jom Raja, the king of the dead. While yogis return to the world to attain immortal status, other simple men face the justice of Jom Raja for their sins. The concept of afterlife among the Santhals indicates both Hindu and Christian influence.

### THE SANTHAL LANGUAGE

The Santhals are an ethnic Munda group and the largest tribe in Jharkhand and West Bengal. They are also found in parts of Odisha, Bihar, Assam and Tripura. Santhali is the language spoken by the Santhals, who also have their own script named Ol Chiki, which is included in the Eighth Schedule to the Indian Constitution. Ol-Chiki is also the medium of instruction in many schools today.

Folk dance performed by the Santhal people

Santhal masks

Wall decoration of a Santhal hut

# 7

# OCCUPATIONAL RITUALS

Perform all work carefully, guided by compassion.

– ***Veda Vyasa***

## COMMUNITY FISHING

Several interesting and amazing occupational rituals are observed in India. The Angami tribe of Nagaland practises a distinctive form of community fishing called *tsüngremmong*, which has the entire community working together to catch fish. The Angamis believe that this practice leads to good luck and prosperity for the entire community, apart from a mouthwatering dinner, of course.

## BLOWPIPE HUNTERS

The Konyak tribe of Nagaland has a unique hunting method using blowpipes. In this traditional method of hunting, they use small darts made of cane or bamboo, which are blown through blowpipes to bring down small animals like birds and squirrels. Recent conservation efforts in the jungles have now decreased this hunting ritual.

## THE KONYAK HEADHUNTERS

The Konyak Nagas or the Konyak tribe of Nagaland were a notorious ethnic group known for their fearsome headhunting practices and elaborate facial tattoos. This warrior tribe used to decapitate the heads of their enemies in battle and fetch them to their village as trophies. The practice of headhunting went on until the 1970s before it was banned. Today only a few of these fierce headhunters are alive, albeit inactive. Hunting was their main occupation and each male child in the family had a weapon reserved for him. Weapons like daos, bows and arrows, spears and guns were utilized by the Konyaks to hunt animals. But there were some animals that were normally not hunted by the Konyaks. These were mainly the 'spirit animals'. Hunting them was considered inauspicious and the harbinger of bad omens.

For the uninitiated, headhunting is the practice of severing and preserving a decapitated head.

Can you see the animal skulls on the wall?

### A Brief History of the Konyak Nagas

Earlier, the Konyak tribe of Nagaland was divided into groups with separate ethnic entities. These groups were then distinguishable from each other according to their geographical locations, tattoo patterns and language. The British were the ones to coin the term *Konyak* and group all of them under a single name.

The Konyak tribe is a part of the mongoloid race and is believed by historians to have migrated to their present home in Mon District of Nagaland from the east after crossing the Patkai Hills. The battle-loving and fierce nature of the Konyak Naga tribe was responsible for their isolation from the rest of the world for a long stretch of time. In the early twentieth century, the arrival of the British in

India was largely responsible for the Konyaks to gradually touch base with the outside world.

Mon District, the home of the Konyaks, is also called the Land of Anghs. The *angh* is the monarch or chief of the Konyak village and his tribe. Each Konyak village boasts of an angh. But there are nine special villages that are the strongest among the Konyak Nagas, and their chiefs are the most powerful anghs. The lineage of these nine anghs is also known as *angh-tak* and is considered the highest noble family among the Konyaks. These nine villages are Chi, Mon, Longwa, Sheanghah Chingyu, Shangnyu, Longzang, Tang, Yansha and Zangkham. All nine villages follow the hereditary transfer of power of the anghs, where only the son of the angh can be the next angh. It is mandatory for the *angh-tak* of a village to marry an *anghya*, the daughter of another angh-tak from one of the other eight villages. This marriage is a powerful alliance formed between two influential villages. Only the children born to this anghya have the right to be future anghs. The eldest son normally has the right. However, this transfer of power is hereditary only in the northern part of Mon District, which is also called the Lower Konyak area. In the southern part of Mon, also known as the Upper Konyak area, power is not hereditary. In the Upper Konyak area, the social system is autocratic. The angh has to earn his power here through status, prestige, wealth and valour instead of just the privilege of birth. The *angh-tak* also has special privileges in Konyak society, like the option of taking other lovers and concubines other than his anghya. However, the children born to these other wives do not have a claim to the angh's property.

But why would the Konyak tribe cut off the heads of their enemies? They firmly believed, for starters, that the skull possessed all the soul force and power of the being. This soul force was also considered responsible for the overall prosperity and fertility of the land, abundant crops in a successful harvest and the general wealth and well-being of the Konyak villagers. This is why all the skulls brought to the village were kept at designated places. Normally, animal skulls were kept at the homes of the individuals who hunted them. And enemy skulls were seen hanging on the walls of the angh's house and the *morungs*. Morungs were the dormitories where bachelor males of the tribe lived together. Boys entered the morungs at a young age to reside there and learn hunting, farming and other ways of life from their elders. These young boys got their first tattoos done in the morungs. However, once married, they had to leave the morung and move into a house.

Rituals were conducted before the warriors embarked on their headhunting journey, followed by many others after their victorious return. The tribe members sang songs and performed dances to welcome their heroes with many heads. The Konyak hunter had this strange belief that by severing and winning the head of an enemy, he had also secured the services of the victim in the afterlife. The number of heads one severed meant the number of slaves one had in the afterlife. The Konyaks headhunted to inaugurate a morung or sometimes just a new long drum, strange as it may sound.

## THE BLACK-AND-WHITE MAGICAL RITUALS OF THE BAIGAS

The meaning of *baiga* is 'sorcerer'. According to the mythology of the Baiga tribe of Madhya Pradesh, they created the Indian race. Nanga (nude) Baiga was the Indian Adam and Nangi (nude) Baigin was the Indian Eve. By this theory, God crafted this tribe with his own hands much before other human beings were created. Nanga Baiga was also reputed to be a great and powerful wizard armed with potent charms. His right shoulder was responsible for the creation of white magic, while he created black magic with his left shoulder. The lifestyle, rituals and customs of the Baigas revolve around these magical beliefs. The tribe holds omens and superstitions in high esteem, which influence several life choices of the tribe members. Some of the good omens for the Baigas are women, cows, tigers, full pitchers of water and corpses while the bad omens consist of men, ghosts and empty pitchers of water, to name a few. The most powerful magicians and sorcerers among the Baigas are called *dewar*s, and doctors for humans and animals are called *gunia*s. Body tattoos replace ornaments in their culture, and the tattoo process is known as *godnaharin*. Song and dance have both cultural and ritualistic significance in the Baiga community. They are known for their Karma dance and other dances like Saila, Reena, Sua, Tapadi and Dadaria. Baigas have a unique method of fishing where they dam streams to source fish. Panthers are killed with a single blow by Baiga hunters. That's magical hunting for you!

### The Baiga: A Brief Overview

The Baiga tribe is among the vulnerable tribes of India. Though they have a weak presence in parts of Odisha, Chhattisgarh, Jharkhand, UP, MP and West Bengal, they belong to Bihar. Traditionally, they lived a semi-nomadic life and engaged in slash-and-burn cultivation. But now they live in the forested parts of Bihar and rely majorly on the forest and its produce for their survival.

## THE SORCERERS OF THE NILGIRIS

The Kurumba tribe, hailing from the mid-ranges of the Nilgiris in Tamil Nadu, is certainly unique as they are experts on sorcery and magic. The Kurumbas are thought to be the descendants of the seventh-century Pallavas and practise shifting cultivation and trapping and hunting small animals and birds. Beautiful works of art are created by the male temple workers. The traditional music of the Kurumba uses bamboo pipes called *kolu* and *bugiri* and drums named *tambette*. But the Kurumbas are primarily known for sorcery. So entrenched are their powers of sorcery in the minds of the other tribes that sickness and death are considered to be spells cast by the Kurumba. The people in charge of Kurumba magic and sorcery are the diviner or the *kanigara*, the exorcist or the *devvagara*, and the sorcerer or *odia*. These gentleman are aided by nature, from where they source their potent herbs, spells and roots. The therapist, or *maddugara*, is the one who cures, while the wizard, or *pilligara*, has supernatural powers and is believed to be capable of transforming himself into any animal of his choice.

In the 1800s, suspected supernatural Kurumba deeds of sorcery led to the other tribes in the Nilgiris uniting and retaliating against them. Several massacres of the Kurumba were reported. Kurumba men are essentially hunters, cultivators and gatherers, while the Kurumba women have traditionally been body tattooists. The Kurumbas were also known as healers because of their impressive knowledge of medicinal plants. The most important element for this tribe is honey. They collect and preserve it because it is useful in the use of several medicines they make.

## THE WILD HONEY COLLECTORS

Both Jarawa men and women of the Andamans collect wild honey from the tall trees on the islands. While they collect honey, the Jarawa sing songs to express their happiness at acquiring this delicacy. The honey collector chews the sap from the leaves of a bee-repellent plant, such as ooyekwalin. Then they spray repellent with their mouths towards the bees to keep them away. Once the bees have disappeared, the Jarawas cut the bee's nest, which they place in a wooden bucket that's on their backs. The Jarawa always have a bath as a ritual after consuming honey.

### THE TRIBES OF THE ANDAMAN ISLANDS

The other major tribes of the Andaman Islands, apart from the Jarawas, include the Onge, Great Andamanese, Sentinelese, Shompen and Nicobarese among others. These tribes are thought to have lived in their Indian Ocean home for up to 55,000 years! The thousands of Indians who have settled on the islands have outnumbered these tribes now. This abrupt contact with outsiders over the past decades is often seen as a threat of extinction of these tribes. Per the 2011 Census, only 380 Jarwas are found today. Except Nicobarese, all other tribes are less than 500 in number. It has been more than a hundred years since any signs of occupation of the Jangil tribe was seen.

## THE PERFECT BLEND OF HINDUISM AND ISLAM: THE MEO PEOPLE

The Meo people of Haryana are a perfect blend of Hinduism and Islam, demonstrating how diverse religious practices can peacefully coexist in a single community. The Meos are a Rajput caste as well as a Muslim community.

At a Meo wedding, one will get to see the Islamic *nikah* ceremony, paying *mehr* (bride price), and so on. They maintain a Hindu-like kinship pattern – like Hindus the Meos also wouldn't marry within the same gotra. They also observe Hindu-style engagement rituals. When child marriage was common, the Meos also celebrated *gauna* – a north-Indian Hindu ritual that marked the bride's entry into the groom's house for the consummation of marriage after the bride would come of age. Until then, the child bride would live with her parents.

They were originally livestock farmers but have evolved to take up various other occupations thanks to urban influence and exposure to modern lifestyles.

The Meos are now owners of trucking businesses, serve in the army or police and work as daily wage labourers, plumbers, electricians, basket traders, money lenders and what not. A large number of the Meos also depend on agriculture.

## THE MUSICAL NOMADS

The traditional occupation of the nomadic Kalbelia people from Rajasthan was catching snakes and then trading their venom for other commodities. The Wildlife Protection Act of 1972 put a stop to snake handling. Today they travel a great distance for work and are distinguished thanks to their colourful dance performances, which are the forte of the women of this tribe. This is a sensuous form of folk dance, with swirling, graceful movements that make this dance a visual treat. Men participate by playing musical instruments like the *pungi*, which is a woodwind instrument. From costumes to the dance movements, the theme of snakes can't be missed in whatever they do.

So, needless to say, the Kalbelias still worship snakes. And despite being otherwise a Hindu tribe, they bury their dead.

## THE UNIQUE HOMES OF THE CHANGPA TRIBE

The Changthang Plateau in Ladakh has a nomadic pastoral tribe that's truly unique. The lofty snow-covered mountains of Jammu and Kashmir are where the Changpas have made their home as they depend on the resources of the mountains for their survival. The hills also shape their unique rituals and culture. One of their occupations is cultivating barley on the hilly slopes. But they are also great traders as they gather salt from the northern shores of the Tsokar Lake in the Rupshu region and sell it in Ladakh. They make products by rearing cattle and from their flocks of pashmina goats. The Changpas reside in beautiful tents that they create from goat and yak hair, using their natural surroundings optimally and with great perfection. The traditional Changpa tent, called *rebo*, is made of yak wool. Weaving these tents is a slow and painstaking process, which takes months to complete. But once this is done, the rebo survives for long periods and is used by one generation and the next. They are rarely discarded. When a part of the rebo wears off, it is simply repaired. A rectangular portion is cut off and a newly woven segment is stitched into the tent.

The pastoral tribe follows Buddhism and perform purification rituals. They migrate four times a year and each time, they wear their best clothes. They must wear a fancy headdress and nice shoes before they start off.

### The Royal Fabric

Pashmina has been regarded as a royal fabric for a long time. The Mughal emperor Akbar was a great admirer of pashmina, and he introduced the concept of *dushala*, a method of double weaving where both sides of the shawl can be used. Akbar also exported it to the Ottoman Empire in the sixteenth century, where it became a rage by the eighteenth century. The French emperor Napoleon Bonaparte was so enamoured by pashmina that he had made a gift of this to his wife Josephine.

Every family of the rebo household, among all the four tribes, has to adhere to complex protocols and superstitions. The tent is divided into two spheres according to gender, with the stove placed in the centre of the rebo. The left of the rebo is the woman's domain, where food and utensils are stored, and this is where the kitchen is. To the right is the male's domain, where the men sit and also store their supplies like saddles and riding gear. In a typically patriarchal move, males are allowed access to both the right and left sides of the rebo, but females rarely ever come into the right half of the tent or the male domain. However, the rebo is the nucleus of a Changpa home, and the stove keeps the home warm. The Changpas eat, sleep and socialize sitting or lying on a woven yak or sheep wool rug placed around the stove.

## THE MAGICAL KORKUS

Magic is a common practice among the Korkus, who believe in ghosts and black magic. They take the help of the *parihar* to control the ghosts that haunt them.

The Parihar, in turn, takes the help of some mantras, which involve a sacred formula, tantrums (cult) and a few wild roots to bid goodbye to these ghosts. Besides the parihar, there are a select few who are aware of this secret ghostbusting practice. When the parihar is absent, the help of these people is taken to subdue the ghosts. Through this secret practice, spells are uttered by blowing air through the mouth, known as *jhad phuk* in the local lingo. This practice supposedly serves as a remedy for several diseases like fever and headache. The Korkus prefer the parihar to cure illnesses instead of engaging the service of doctors. A Korku who is well-versed in the art of *jantar mantar* is believed to have the power to cause someone's death by merely punching on his name. Women who indulge in this strange practice are called *bhagto-dukri*.

> The *Parihar* refers to the traditional system of self-governance in the Korku community which is called *Chavadi Swashasan*. All village issues are resolved by the community and the *Parihar* is led by a member called an *Aada Patel*.

Some of the blind and wild beliefs of the Korkus are as follows:

- When they get tired of heavy and incessant rain, the Korkus attempt to stop the rain by making a naked boy catch a frog and bury it alive.

- To ascertain if a new village is prosperous, a wooden cup is filled with millet to the brim and left to rest for the night. The next morning, the grain is poured out and measured. If the grains fill the cup and run over, it is considered a sign of prosperity. However, if this doesn't happen, it is indicative of an evil omen.
- To protect children from cold, goitre, sore eyes and lingering diseases, a scarlet thread is tied around their necks as a protective charm. The Korkus consider Acheri as their disease spirit. Acheri is rather bullish as he supposedly attacks the wearer of red garments.
- The Korkus are supposedly capable of transferring their disease to others by employing their magical practices. The person who does this simply catches hold of the latter's cloth and draws two images, the first upright and the other upside down. When the person wears this cloth, he is infected by the disease.
- They make offerings to Baghdeo, the tiger god, to protect the village from a tiger's entry.

### The Korku: A Brief Overview

The Korku tribe has a strong presence in central India. They can be found mainly in Khandwa, Betul, Burhanpur and Chhindwara districts of Madhya Pradesh (MP), Chhattisgarh and some adjoining parts of Maharashtra. These people fashion their huts from grass and wood and prefer living in small groups. A small storage place stands in front of every Korku house, where cattle feed and farm produce are stored. Since the early days, the Korkus have worked as cultivators of the land with a love for forests.

They are expert agriculturists and are considered pioneers of coffee and potato cultivation.

## THE BLITHE BAIGAS

The Baigas of Bihar build their houses with bamboo and other household items like baskets. They love fresh honey and use traditional techniques to collect it from the forest. The Baigas are also experts when it comes to making folk medicines thanks to their detailed knowledge of wild medicinal plants and shrubs. Their rich cultural heritage reflects their unique dance form, music and dramas. This tribe follows a unique ritual in which the entire family has to leave their house and build a new one after the death of a family member. Thank God, they don't use bricks and cement to build their houses! The Baigas also have a tattoo tradition. It is mandatory for everyone to get their body parts tattooed at a certain age and on a certain occasion.

## REINCARNATION THEORIES

The Bison-Horn Maria tribe believes strongly in reincarnation, which is the cycle of death and rebirth. As a result, most of their rituals are centred on this theme. As soon as a child is born, the first thing that the villagers do is to examine the infant's body. They believe that an ancestor is being incarnated, and the child's body will bear similar marks to the body of this ancestor. No wonder medicine men are so powerful in these tribal villages because of these beliefs. Strange and legendary tales about the spiritual and physical powers of these medicine men have survived years of oral narration.

## The Tribe with the Bison Horn

Bison-Horn Maria derives its name from its remarkable and eye-catching headdress that's made from wild bison and adorned with peacock feathers. The wild bison is now an extinct species, but these people use their already existing skulls to wear during wedding ceremonies and other special functions. The new-age headdress is made from cattle horns. Bison-Horn Maria men also stand out because of their long ponytails, which are meticulously maintained as each man carries a special comb by attaching it to his loincloth. Women are clad in just white skirts, leaving their upper bodies bare. They use several kinds of jewellery to adorn themselves. The Bison-Horn Maria men also carry a tobacco box in their loincloth. Apart from tobacco addiction, they love *landa*, a kind of rice beer. Landa is consumed religiously at all festivals and special occasions. The intoxication often leads to violence and even murder among the Bison-Horn Maria. Alcohol kills!

Bison-horn Marias performing folk dance in Jagdalpur, Bastar, Chhattisgarh

The villages of the Bison-Horn Maria are made up of many hamlets surrounded by strong fences. Each house has three rooms, a thatched roof and walls made of woven bamboo. Each side of the house has a shed that serves as a home for cattle and a pigsty. A house is built specifically for travellers and is located near the home of the village headman. The outskirts of every village have the god of the clan enshrined. The Bison-Horn Maria worship several gods, and each clan god is territorial but is related to the other clan gods. These clan gods supposedly protect the village and aid in identifying and exposing black magic within the village.

### The Bison-Horn Maria: Where to Find Them

The Bison-Horn Maria is an introverted tribe mainly found in the Bastar region of Chhattisgarh and in some parts of Madhya Pradesh and Maharashtra. By choice, this tribe has chosen to stay in the dense forests instead of in a so-called civilized society. The tribe practises shifting cultivation and depends on forest produce for their survival.

## DHANGERS

According to Dhangar legend, they were created from the dust of Lord Shiva's body. It is also believed that this tribe migrated from Gujarat to Goa. However, it is easy to identify members of this tribe from other communities in this region because of their unique attire and occupation. These tribals are mostly cattle herders or shepherds who prefer a semi-nomadic lifestyle. They always carry a stick when they go cattle grazing and are watched by either one or a couple of hunter dogs. Religious rituals include the worship of their local god Bira Deva. Polygamy is a common practice among the Dhangars, and money, property or valuables can be paid by the groom as bride price (also called bride wealth).

## THE EXCLUSIVE MEDICINE MAN

The medicine man or the herbalist among the Lepchas of Sikkim is called *maon-doak*. Using his knowledge of medicinal plants, the maon-doak makes medicine to tackle the several health problems of the tribe, like bone fractures and snakebites. However, this herbalist restricts his medicinal practices and prescriptions exclusively for the benefit of the Lepcha community. Everyone else is considered a foreigner, and outsiders are not given the same treatment. So make sure you carry your own medicines when you pay the Lepchas a visit.

The maon-doak believes that the plants that he uses to make medicines will produce adverse effects if he shares his traditional knowledge with outsiders. The Lepchas would then have to face the wrath of the supreme deity of the medicinal plants. Experts believe that this possessiveness and reluctance to share traditional knowledge has gradually led to a sharp decline of ancient herbal practices within the Lepcha community.

A Lepcha child

# 8

# STRANGE RITUALS

India lives in several centuries at the same time.

– ***Arundhati Roy***

## LOST IN TRANSLATION

The language spoken by the Garo tribe belongs to the Bodo-Garo languages branch of the Tibeto-Burman language family. It is believed that the written language of the Garo was lost when mass migration took place to the present-day Garo Hills. The Garo language/script was strangely written on the skins of their cows for memory retention. In their defence, they probably lacked writing paper when they were on the run. However, the acute shortage of food and famines experienced during the migration forced the Garo ancestors to cook and eat these cows. So the written language script was lost, and there was no chance of retrieval as the Garos literally gobbled up their own language.

### ASSAMESE TRIBE IN FOCUS: THE GARO TRIBE

The Garo tribe of Assam is known for its vibrant culture and colourful lifestyle. The Garos were early immigrants to this land and originated from the Garo Hills of Meghalaya and then settled at various places around it. During the early nineteenth century, the Garo migrated from the Garo Hills to the other neighbouring states that make up the Seven Sisters of India. The Wangala Festival is one of the main festivals of the Garo tribe and is celebrated with pride and gusto. This vibrant festival takes place after the harvest of the first crop of the year. The Garos wear colourful dresses and dance to their traditional music during the festival.

## KIDNAPPED

Ziro in Arunachal Pradesh is home to the Apatanis, who are one of the few tribes in the world that worship nature. The Apatanis are also known for their colourful festivals, beautiful handloom designs, exquisite cane and bamboo crafts and wonderful methods of sustainable farming and social forestry. Social order is maintained by the vibrant traditional village councils called *bulyañ*.

Once upon a time, Apatani women were considered the most beautiful in all of Arunachal Pradesh. In the olden days, men belonging to other tribes would often steal the Apatani women and make them their wives. This led the Apatani men to take an extreme step that is reflective of patriarchy at its highest level. Instead of rising to the occasion and fighting to protect their women, the Apatani men tattooed the faces of their women and insisted that they wear massive nose plugs, to make them less appealing, attractive or beautiful to be kidnapped by the men from other tribes. This crazy ritual of beauty and the beast does not exist today thankfully. However, the older Apatani women can still be spotted sporting facial tattoos and massive nose rings. Old habits die hard!

## THE TATTOO TRIBE

Almost all the tribes of Nagaland practised headhunting, although the Konyak Nagas earned a fearsome reputation thanks to their bloody headcount. However, it is their tattoos that make the Konyak tribe unique. The Konyak tribe is often called the face tattoo tribe of Nagaland. The tattoos on the bodies of the Konyaks were like an identification mark or ornamentation. These body tattoos segregated a child from an adult and a warrior from a farmer. Women also sported body tattoos, which were used to distinguish an aristocratic Konyak lady from other women or an unmarried woman from a married one. These body tattoos reflected a person's maturity and the transition from one stage of life to another. A common belief that existed was that tattoos would ensure a safe passage to the afterlife after death. Hence, almost all the Konyaks had tattoos. However, facial tattoos are the most fascinating part of the Konyak Naga tribe. Only a warrior capable of fetching a severed head to the village was entitled to get a facial tattoo done, as this was a mark of the best warriors of the land. Thus, the rituals of headhunting and tattooing were seamlessly linked. There were several other reasons for getting a body tattoo. Tattoos on the chest depicted the different stages of life. A young Konyak girl would get a tattoo done on the calves of her legs. When a young woman was about to get married, she got a tattoo done on her knees. However, only a lady of noble origin could get a tattoo done on their arms or neck.

It is interesting to note that the tattoos were done only by women tattoo artists among the Konyaks. These women belonged to the noble families of the anghs, and only the Anghyas (wives of anghs, or the chiefs) were allowed to tattoo the bodies of the Konyak men. This art and ritual of tattoo-making was passed on from mother to daughter. When they married and moved to other villages, they took their designs and expertise with them. Normally, the ladies would first make the tattoos on other girls as a form of practice before they would draw tattoos on the men. But the Konyaks also had male tattoo artists with specialized job functions. They only did rare forms of tattoos, like the tattoos of the tiger spirit, which were usually drawn on the backs of the most powerful anghs. There was the *shen-tu* (face tattoo), *tangta-tu* (body tattoo) and *kong-tu* (nose tattoo), and each had their personal folktales and songs. To draw a tattoo, or *tu*, one has to prick the skin with a rattan thorn. The pigment used for tattooing used to come from the *kong* tree (red cedar), which oozes a type of sap known as the *ying tee*.

### THE ANGH AND HIS PENIS TATTOO

Yes, you read that right! An angh used to have tattoo done on his penis! Angh Chakwang of Longzang village was one of the most powerful and fiercest headhunters in India. His headhunting prowess was so remarkable that his entire body was covered with tattoos.

This angh had severed so many heads that there was no more space on his body for tattoos. Only his penis was not inked. To mark his status as the greatest headhunter of all time, our man decided to get a penis tattoo done after some deliberation, thus making him the only person with this rare penis tattoo. He was rumoured to have as many as thirty wives, five of whom had blue blood. This angh clearly believed in the theory of excess. Eleven of his wives were given the task of creating his penis tattoo. Ouch! Wonder if that's a world record!

## TATTOO TECHNIQUES

Konyak tattoos were made using a handcrafted comb. These combs were created from rattan palm spikes that were bound together by plant fibres. The two techniques of Konyak tattoos were hand tapping and hand hammering. The comb was dipped in a special ink made from the resin of the *Toona ciliata* tree and then tapped with another tool or hammered on the skin continuously until the patterns were created. This was a painful process for sure, especially as the Konyaks had a strict deadline of finishing the process of tattooing in a single day as there were probably heads to be hunted the next day. But the day any Konyak Naga was inked was considered important enough to be celebrated with a grand feast. The women cooked sticky rice, and an animal was killed to go along with it. This extravagant meal was washed down with plenty of rice beer.

## THE END OF HEADHUNTING AND TATTOOING

In 1935, the British officially banned the practice of headhunting in Nagaland. In the British-administered areas, the practice stopped completely. However, in the unadministered areas, it continued till as late as the 1970s. However, the arrival of Christian missionaries in Nagaland in the 1940s finally put an end to headhunting once and for all. The introduction of a new religion and modern education introduced by these missionaries had a calming effect on the headhunting tribes, which slowly led to a massive transition in the Naga lifestyle. The missionaries successfully propagated that tattooing was a heathen practice. Finally, in 1960, the powerful Konyak Student Union officially passed a resolution that stopped the practice of tattooing totally. Despite this, flickers of the final flame burned as tattooing took place even in the late 1970s, before it was banned.

## TEETH BLACKENING

A Konyak chief with his black teeth

Teeth blackening was an individual choice of the Konyaks. Black teeth signified sexual maturity, a sign of beautification and was also followed to prevent tooth decay. The process of blackening their teeth would begin by heating an iron machete over fire and collecting the soot. This black soot was then applied to the teeth as a daily ritual until the staining became permanent. It is just like we brush our teeth every day, except that it is an attempt at whitening for us, unlike the Konyak Naga.

## PULI KALI: THE PLAY OF THE TIGERS

The amazingly strange dance ritual of Puli Kali is performed in Thrissur, Kerala, as a part of Onam, which is a twelve-day celebration in August or September to celebrate the harvest. On the fourth day of Onam, trained artists perform this amazing dance ritual, painted like tigers in resplendent shades of yellow, red, white and black. The accompanying music is that of traditional beats with instruments like the *udukku* and *thakil*. The artists twist and turn to mimic the moves of tigers. Themes of this unique ritual include the tiger being stalked by a hunter or its hunts in the jungle, which are performed with great gusto. This ritual is popular and is greeted with applause and praise from locals and tourists in God's own country.

## MADEY SNANA: KARNATAKA

The ritual of *madey snana*, or spit bath, takes place in Karnataka and was banned in 2010. This is because it highlights the evils of the caste system, which still exist in certain parts of rural India. The Kukke Subramania Temple in Karnataka witnesses a peculiar scene when people from the 'lower castes' roll on the floor over the leftover banana plates of the brahmins, the 'higher castes', after they have finished their meal. This is supposed to cure the rollers of their bodily ailments. The banning of this ritual led to widespread protests from the Malekudiya people, which clearly doesn't believe in the healing powers of modern medicine. As a result, this strange practice or ritual was strangely revoked in 2011. The ban lasted only for a year.

## TOSSING INFANTS FROM THE ROOF

This strange and shocking ritual is practised in two places in Maharashtra and Karnataka. Both Hindus and Muslims participate in this bizarre ritual, which is supposed to bring about a swing in the fortunes of the family. The method used is definitely dubious as infants are tossed below from a height of 50 feet to land in a thick sheet held by men waiting below. The two sites where this is practised are the Baba Umer Dargah near Sholapur, Maharashtra, and Sri Santeswar Temple near Indi, Karnataka. This particular ritual has been taking place for more than 700 years, and no injuries have been reported so far.

## THE BANI FESTIVAL: ANDHRA PRADESH

The Devaragattu Temple located in Kurnool, Andhra Pradesh, celebrates the Bani Festival on a full-moon day in the month of Ashvin (September–October) in the Hindu calendar. This is a dangerous ritual that has devotees thrashing each other with lathis to celebrate Lord Shiva killing a demon. Why they thrash each other instead of demons is anybody's guess! The ritual is over a hundred years old according to the temple priests. During this strange and bloody ritual, medical attendants and the police are deployed to ensure that no one is hurt seriously. The ritual begins late at night and continues till daybreak. Amazingly, and thankfully, there have been no deaths in this violent ritual to date. Things were certainly different during ancient times when this ritual involved the use of axes and spears. But that's a different story!

## THE FESTIVAL OF STONES

The *Pathron Ka Mela*, or the Festival of Stones, in Uttarakhand brings cheer and joy but also puts several lives at risk because of the unique and dangerous ritual that accompanies it. This tradition takes place normally a day after Diwali and involves the villagers from two different villages literally pelting each other with stones. Everybody must get stoned! This is done to celebrate and offer a sacrifice to Goddess Kali. The injured ones are the chosen ones, as their blood is used to smear a tika on the forehead of the idol of the goddess. The animosity of the Halog and Jamog regions of Uttarakhand has given rise to this festival. Legend has it that a girl from Halog was engaged to the prince of Rangioli. She committed sati by burning herself on the funeral pyre of her fiancé, who was poisoned by some evil men of Jamog. This resulted in a fight between the people of Halog and Jamog, and fisticuffs were replaced by stones. Since then, although the enmity has diminished somewhat, the ritual of stone pelting is still observed to recreate the legend and please Goddess Kali with the offering of blood.

## LATH MAR HOLI: UTTAR PRADESH

Holi, the festival of colours, is very popular in India. But a slightly twisted version of Holi takes place in a certain holy region in Uttar Pradesh, where sticks replace colours. The Lath Mar Holi is a unique mix of bamboo sticks, intoxicating herbal drinks and a great deal of thrashing with the sticks at hand. This grand spectacle takes place in Barsana and Nandgaon (the birthplace of Lord Krishna) in Uttar Pradesh about a week before the actual Holi Festival. It attracts journalists and photographers from across the world. The rituals of this weird festival begin with the consumption of bhang, an intoxicating paste made from cannabis mixed with milk and spices, by the male villagers. Then the legend behind this festival is recreated at the local square, where married women beat the intoxicated men with bamboo sticks while they protect themselves from the thrashing with shields. The legend behind this unique ritual can be traced back to when Lord Krishna visited Radha's village, Barsana, from Nandgaon with his friends. Lord Krishna and his gang of boys would playfully tease Radha and her friends, who would thrash them with bamboo sticks and drive them away from the village. Lath Mar Holi has remained a constant in our ever-changing world.

Lath Mar Holi

## THEEMITHI: TAMIL NADU

The ritual of Theemithi is all about walking on fire and is part of a larger ceremony that continues for more than two months, involving ceremonial worship and performances inspired by the Mahabharata. Theemithi commemorates

Draupadi walking on a bed of fire after the conclusion of the Battle of Kurukshetra in the Mahabharata. Draupadi is believed to have emerged from fire, along with her brother Drishtadyumna, and was unhurt by walking on the bed of fire, a task to prove her fidelity. It's truly amazing to see how the devotees manage to walk this difficult path and emerge unscathed. They believe that by walking on a path of burning coal, all their wishes will be granted. Devotees also do it to ward off evil spirits or as an act of penance. However, in a patriarchal twist to the tale, only men are allowed to walk this strange path. This is strange, as it was a woman who inspired this ritual in the first place. This strange ritual takes place during October and November in Tamil Nadu and has spread to countries like Sri Lanka, Singapore and South Africa as well. Talk about going international in a fiery way!

## THE STRANGE BUNDA FESTIVAL

The Bunda Festival is held in and around the Nirmand region and mostly in the Nurpur Vallery of the Sutlej River in Himachal Pradesh. The area where the ceremony occurs comprises sixteen villages. The rituals of this festival involve choosing a villager to appease Goddess Ambika with a life-risking stunt. If the chosen one succeeds in this Mission Impossible, he becomes super rich as he is given offerings like cash, grains and jewellery, which the local temple collects before the day of the stunt and ritual. Lord Parashuram and Goddess Kali are part of the legends connected with this strange ritual. On D-Day, the rope woven by the chosen one, or the *bheda*, is tied across two hills, one end of which is on an end of a high cliff; the second extends steep into the valley. The bheda then slides down this precarious rope, and if he fails, it is considered a human sacrifice to Goddess Ambika. In case the bheda succeeds, goats are sacrificed to the goddess instead. This ritual supposedly aids the village and the villagers to ward off evil spirits and is held every twelve years on a date decided by the local priest.

## THAIPOOSAM

The festival of Thaipoosam honours Lord Murugan or Kartikeya, the god of war and the eldest son of Lord Shiva and Goddess Parvati. It is celebrated in Tamil Nadu and a few other parts of south India on the full moon during the month of Thai (January–February) and commemorates the time when Goddess Parvati gave Kartikeya a spear to kill the evil demon Soorapadman. Devotees pierce their cheeks and tongues, as well as other parts of their bodies, with hot needles, sharp hooks, lances and skewers. Some devotees are not content with these excessive piercings as they try to pull heavy objects like trucks and tractors with these hooks. The ritual is accompanied by incessant drumming and chanting as the devotees reach a trance-like state.

## HIGH ON RITUALS?

The Bhotiya tribe of Uttarakhand has managed to raise quite a few eyebrows on account of their regular use of marijuana. Calm down as it's mainly for religious reasons (or so they claim). This tribe of shepherds can be found mainly in Uttarakhand, which has the ideal climatic conditions to grow pot. But the ritualistic use of marijuana, instead of recreational purposes by the Bhotiya tribe is what is most interesting. The easily available intoxicant has found its way into the rituals observed by the Bhotiyas. Thanks to intermarriage with Hindus over the decades, the original Buddhist culture of the Bhotiyas has blended into a harmonious co-existence between Tibetan Buddhism and Hinduism and led to the fascinating language Rongba. A blend of marijuana and hashish has also entered the scheme of things because of the influence of Hindu mythology and religious traditions. However, alcohol is strictly forbidden among the Bhotiya. Lord Shiva's association with bhang is famous in Indian mythology. He used it to keep the world safe from his rage. Following Lord Shiva's example, the Bhotiya offer bhang, basically a mixture of ground marijuana leaves in milk, when they celebrate both Holi and Maha Shivaratri.

## THE CAVEMEN WITH RITUALS OF THE STONE AGE

The Cholanaikkan people of Kerala were living in isolation and were untouched by civilization until just fifty years ago. They were first contacted in the late 1960s, and this is when the Cholanaikkan first discovered the modern world. In fact, this tribe was officially unknown till the

1971 census. They received national attention only after 1977. They never even wore clothes when they were first contacted and existed in a complete Stone Age culture. The Cholanaikkans lived off the land and its resources. These cavemen were animists who worshipped ancestral spirits. They also worship trees and an undressed stone with a curved top under a large tree. The most primitive and endangered tribe of Kerala with a population of less than 200 people, they are found only in the Karulai and Chunagathara forest ranges. Their features are more African than Indian, and no genetic profile is available. It is assumed that they are Austro-Asian in origin. These hunters and gatherers reside in rock shelters, caves or crude huts beside brooks. Their caves also have names. They distinguish between two people having the same name by adding the name of the cave before their name. They affix –*nu* to their names. Their language has certain similarities to Dravidian languages. They are strictly vegetarian and have birds and animals only as pets or as a hobby. The marriage customs are interesting, especially if there are too many suitors for one girl. The community then steps in, and competitions are arranged, like climbing up a tree with honeycombs to fetch honey. The one fetching the most honey gets the girl. In the event of a tie, a wrestling match is arranged, where the winner gets the girl. If you think the Stone Age wasn't cool, think again. But the most fascinating thing is how the Cholanaikkans have managed to avoid the urban and conventional ways of life into the last half of the twentieth century.

## GAJAN FESTIVAL

The Gajan Festival is focused on the monsoon and the good harvest it fetches. The agricultural community comes together to worship Lord Shiva and local deities like Neel and Dharmathakur, the god of fertility, to make the spring more fertile. Other rituals include body piercings, hooking the flesh and fire plays, which add more colour to Gajan. Many relate the origin of Gajan to the conversion of Buddhist monks to Hinduism in ancient days. That's why the week-long festival dedicated to Lord Shiva has merged the tantric rituals of Buddhism and severe penance. Gajan is held in the last week of Choitro, the final month of the Bengali calendar.

## CHARAK PUJA

The most fascinating part of the Gajan Festival is Charak Puja. The ritual involves the worship of the *charak* tree as the Charak *sanyasi*s perform severe penance both on a tree and around it. Charak Puja takes place on the eve of Poila Boishakh, or the Bengali New Year. A charak tree is the trunk of a tree without any roots or branches and can stretch to a height of about 30 to 40 feet. For it to qualify as a tree of worship, a straight trunk is required. After being worshipped by priests, the tree is then placed inside a ditch and balanced by bamboo. After this, the sanyasis perform their rituals of penance. After the rituals are complete, the tree is immersed in the river. It is believed that the same tree will visit the same ghat of the river the following year when the sanyasis will fetch it again to the puja ground. The place where the charak tree is installed and worshipped is fenced for protection. Only the sanyasis or devotees performing the act are permitted to enter. The charak tree is also believed to be the home of Ardhnarishwar (half man and half woman), the composite form of Lord Shiva and Goddess Parvati. Hence, an idol or mask of Ardhnarishwar is fixed on the top of the tree before the rituals commence. The god symbolizes the combined power of the male and female.

## HOOKED TO GOD

Another incredibly frightening part of the Gajan Festival is how the sanyasis pierce their bodies with sharp hooks without any apparent cuts or injuries. This bloodless piercing appears almost magical, but the secret to it is years of practice in which the knowledge to pierce bodies without causing damage to the veins and inflicting less pain is obtained. In earlier days, peasants would pierce their tongues with sharp needles to hang their bodies from hooks that hung from wooden structures. In this state of painful suspension, the so-called 'lower caste' would be elevated in the social hierarchy to be hailed as a representative of Lord Shiva by his landlord and the masses. Such painful penance is also supposed to give men the experience of the pain of womanhood, including childbirth, and for them to realize the pain a woman has to go through. The men, held by hooks, would fly in a circular path thanks to the ropes attached to the charak tree on one end and the

Bloodless piercing at Charak festival

hook to the other end. Even if they fell from a height at times, no one faced serious injuries. There are instances of mothers hanging from these hooks, allowing devotees to embrace their infants. This is supposed to usher in good luck and ensure the well-being of the infants. In extreme cases, devotees lie on sharp nails laid on a studded plank or climb onto a bamboo platform adorned with a bed of thorns. Sometimes, their bodies are pierced with arrows with their tips wrapped with cotton, which are set on fire.

## THE LAST ARYANS OF LADAKH

Around 200 km from Leh, the capital of Ladkah, a group of villages rest along the Indus River, about 40 km from the Pakistan border. Until recently, the locals here were isolated from the rest of the world. But their rituals and traditions are centuries old, just like their genetics. However, the origins of the Brokpa tribes are disputed. Some believe these are the last pure Aryans, descendants of the army of Alexander the Great. Others believe them to be the earliest settlers in the Ladakh region, having migrated there thousands of years ago from Pakistan and eastern Afghanistan. The Brokpa tribes are a unique population for sure as their culture, lifestyle, religious practices and appearance differ greatly from the traditional Ladakhi population. Amongst the many villages in the valley, some have a population of only a hundred. The farming communities produce grains, fruit, vegetables and colourful flowers, which are used to adorn their traditional headdress, known as a *tepi*. Flowers are also offered to the deities worshipped in their lineage of Buddhism. Access to the Brokpa population had been limited. Only in the last few decades have they started going to Leh to sell their products, migrating for employment, and have allowed tourists to visit their villages. These villages of Dah, Haanu, Beema, Darchik and Garkon are where the Dard Brokpa community resides.

### Pregnancy Tourism

It is rumoured that European women come to these Aryan villages with the hope of getting impregnated by men believed to be racially pure Aryans. The women reportedly fornicate with local men and then return to their countries with a child of 'pure race'. This story of pregnancy tourism has actually made the Aryan Valley famous in the West. However, locals deny it. It remains a mystery, just like the Alexander connection.

## THE ISOLATED TRIBE

Abhuj Maria is a tribe in Chhattisgarh that has been living in hiding. They live an isolated life and have always shied away from establishing a connection with the modern world. This Gond sub-tribe lives in the isolated regions of Narayanpur Tehsil of Bastar District in Chhattisgarh. This primitive race is also ferocious and is feared by outsiders as they shoot at any intruders with arrows. The tiger is honoured and feared by the Abhuj Marias, who protect the king of the jungle from poachers. They also drink from ponds or rivers, replicating a tiger or a wild animal. The material pleasures of life fail to tempt the Abhuj Maria, who have managed to keep their quintessential tribal culture alive and intact to date. They rarely clean their bodies or wash their clothes. They wear limited clothes, anyway, choosing to cover themselves with just a loin cloth. They like traditional ethnic jewellery and adorn their necks with iron rings. The women are fond of earrings and sometimes pierce their ears with as many as fourteen holes. Divorce and remarriages are common among the Abhuj Maria, but adultery is banned. Marriages among blood relations, including brothers and sisters, are common. A strong sense of community exists within this tribe, and equality and brotherhood are valued principles. The Abhuj Maria engage in slash-and-burn cultivation. Over time, they have also started using other forms of settled cultivation. The main outputs include two types of millets, namely kolha and korsa and rice.

## THE LAW OF GOD

In India, court cases are notorious for dragging on and on for years, bringing stress upon individuals and families, as well as draining their energy and financial resources. The Indian judicial system is reputed for its slow pace and intricate processes. Presenting a new set of rituals that will help you swim against the tide in a sea of legalities. The कोर्ट केस विजय प्राप्ति पूजा (Court Case Vijay Prapti Puja) is a ritual that originated in Jaipur, Rajasthan. This ritual is tailor-made to invoke divine intervention to provide clarity and strength in the minds of those entangled in court cases. This ritual supposedly reduces stress and anxiety and helps one make informed decisions. Be calm and win court cases with this legal ritual. All objections overruled!

# 9

# MISCELLANEOUS RITUALS

But it is I who am the ritual, I the sacrifice, the offering to the ancestors, the healing herb, and the transcendental chant. I am the butter and the fire and the offering.

– ***Bhagavad Gita***

## THE KILA RAIPUR RURAL OLYMPICS: PUNJAB

Raipur District of Punjab hosts an annual festival that has more to do with sports and entertainment than religion. The Kila Raipur Rural Olympics are enjoyed by thousands of local fans, as well as domestic and foreign tourists.

The sheer range of competition on offer is exciting, right from bullock cart races, horse racing, mule carts, shot put, kabaddi, tug of war, tractor race, high jump, long jump and middle-distance racing. Entertainment on offer includes bikers and horsemen performing daredevil stunts and musclemen pulling tractors and trucks with their hair, teeth and ears! After these daytime festivities are over, there is dance and music in the evenings. The Kila Raipur Rural Olympics is testimony to the fact that Punjabis know how to combine their love for sports with fun and entertainment. *Chak de phatte!*

## JALLIKATTU: TAMIL NADU

Jallikattu is a traditional farmer's sport in Tamil Nadu where young men try to grab the prize on offer by taming

Jallikattu

a raging bull and riding it. The bulls for this sport are specially reared, and their horns are sharpened. More men than bulls were injured in this daredevil sport!

## SONEPUR CATTLE FAIR: BIHAR

The Sonepur Cattle Fair takes place in Bihar and is the biggest cattle fair of its kind in Asia. At this annual event, which stretches over fifteen days to one month, a wide variety of animal and bird species are traded. The town of Sonepur rests at the confluence of the rivers Ganga and Gandak. What makes the cattle fair unique and interesting is that many animals that are sold here cannot be traded legally in India. One can get hold of several varieties of farm animals, buffaloes, dog breeds, donkeys, ponies, goats, Persian horses, rabbits and camels. But the star of the cattle fair is the mighty elephant. The special Haathi Bazaar in the fair is well decorated, and here, resplendent elephants are lined up for sale. The trade of so many elephants does not happen anywhere else in the world. The Sonepur Cattle Fair originated during the reign of the founder of the Maurya Empire in ancient India, Chandragupta Maurya (340–297 BCE), who used to purchase horses and elephants across the river Ganges. This amazing cattle fair begins on the full moon day of Kartik Poornima in November.

## PUSHKAR FAIR: RAJASTHAN

The cattle fair held in Pushkar, Rajasthan, lasts for five days and is unique because of the particular focus on the camel. Held during the full moon of Kartik Poornima in November, camels are shaved and decorated specially for this festival, although there are other animals like cows, goats and sheep as well. Traders and farmers bargain to buy livestock, but camels are the main reason they all come there. After the camels are beautified, they are paraded before their prospective owners and also made to participate in races and games to display their prowess and skills. What's more, they even walk the ramp in local beauty contests. Beauty lies in the eyes of the beholder, in this case the camel owner. There is also live entertainment with musicians, dancers, acrobats and magicians, in case you don't have enough moolah to buy a camel. In that case, fear not as you can pick up curios, footwear and fabrics from stalls at the fair, which are comparatively cheaper.

## THE BUFFALO TRIBE OF THE NILGIRI HILLS

Another tribe that's believed to have descended from Alexander's Macedonian army which invaded India as early as 327 BCE are the Todas of Tamil Nadu. Their rituals include worshiping hill gods, including Lord Amodr and Goddess Teikirizi. The Todas rely on cattle for their livelihood as they produce milk products, but some of them have also become expert silversmiths. The buffalo is the centre of all religious rituals of the Todas, and these rituals are mandatory for almost every single dairy activity, right from milking to churning butter to shifting pastures with the seasons to feeding the herds with salt. Ritualistic ceremonies also exist when dairymen–priests are ordained or when dairies are rebuilt or for re-thatching funerary Toda temples. The months when these rites and complex funeral rituals take place are also considered favourable for sexual intercourse among the Todas, and poetic songs dedicated to the buffalo cult are composed and chanted to commemorate this sexual union. Polyandry is pretty common among the Todas, and several men may have a common wife, although brothers usually engage in this practice. But when a Toda woman is pregnant, one of her husbands ceremonially gives her a toy bow and arrow, thus declaring himself as the social father of her child.

## THE RITUALS OF THE WATER TRIBE

The Koya people of Andhra Pradesh believes that they came out of water. Koya mythology states that the origin of life is water, and the friction between the fourteen seas caused the birth of creatures like moss, toads, fish and saints. God was the last saint to be born, and he created the *tuniki* and *regu* fruits first before he created man and woman. The multiracial and multilingual Koya community has a strong relationship with nature. They don't just live off nature; they live because of it. The association of birth with water is present in the marriage rituals of the Koyas too. Water, considered the symbol of fertility, is poured on a new bride; this is obviously done to make her fertile. Another interesting Koya tradition is observed during social and religious occasions. An intoxicating drink named *ippa sara* or the *mohuva* (mahua) drink gives the Koyas much-needed refreshment and relief after a hard day's work. Customary laws of the Koyas state that natural resources must have communal ownership. The *pedda*, or the village headman, oversees social, political and religious activities. The Koyas have their own ethnic religion, but they also worship several Hindu gods and goddesses. They have many female deities, and Mother Earth is the most important among them. The main Koya festivals are Vijji Pandum, the seeds charming festival, and KondalaKolupu, the festival to appease the hill deities. The Koyas perform a colourful dance called *Permakok*, or the bison horn dance, during their festivals and marriage ceremonies. They live in the forests, plains and valleys on both sides of the Godavari River and can be mostly found in Andhra Pradesh, Telangana, Chhattisgarh and Odisha. They are believed to have migrated to central India from their original home in Bastar in present-day Chhattisgarh. The Koyas have five sub-divisions called *gotrams*. Each Koya is born into a clan, and he cannot leave it under any circumstances. The Koyas have a patrilineal and patrilocal family structure, and the family is known as *kutum*. They have nuclear families and follow monogamy. The Koyas stock community funds and grain banks to help needy families and provide food security for the entire tribe. They either bury or cremate their dead and also erect menhirs in their memory.

## LOVE FOR THE ENVIRONMENT

The Gond community of Chhattisgarh is one of India's largest tribes and is amazingly connected to nature. Gond dead bodies were previously cremated, with the corpse placed atop a pile of wood and burned to ash. However, the Gonds had to make a crucial decision when they were caught in a catch-22 situation. They had to make a choice between continuing an ancient ritual and protecting their natural environment, which they consider sacred. So the Gonds of Chhattisgarh decided to bury their dead instead of cremating them. This decision was taken to save trees in an unusual departure from their ancient Hindu ritual of burning the dead. This love for the environment that transcends everything else is largely because the Gond tribes depend on the forest for their basic survival and existence. The forest and its trees provide shelter, medicines, water, food and fuel. Then there is the sacred angle as well.

## BONDA FASHION

The Bondas of Odisha have a unique style of dressing. The women are semi-clad but wear different sorts of rings, necklaces and jewellery around their bodies. They also wear bangles on their arms and metal rings that cover their necks. Bonda women hunt and look for food in the deep forest, and their ornaments also serve to protect them from injuries and attacks by wild animals apart from the beautification angle. Bonda women have shaved heads, and they wear two types of headbands, called *turuba* and *lobeda*. The turuba is made of grass, and the lobeda is made of beads. Worn together, the turuba secures the lobeda and protects the beaded headband from slipping off the head. Bonda women wear metal bands of aluminium, called *khagla*, and necklaces made of beads, called *mali*, around their necks. Because of the *ringa* cloth that covers the women from the waist down, the khagla and mali serve as clothing for the upper body. Both men and women wear brass earrings, called *limbi*, and aluminium rings on their fingers, called *orti*. Bachelors or newly married men must wear their own set of ornaments. When males are eight or nine years old, they wear headbands called *ornaghboh*, bangles called *sungrai*, necklaces called *thangimali*, earrings called *unsurul* and rings called *sabah*. After marriage, the men do not adorn their bodies with any more ornaments.

## THE COURTROOM RITUAL MADE FAMOUS BY BOLLYWOOD

Indian courtrooms have long discontinued the ritual of having witnesses take an oath by placing their hands on the Bhagavad Gita or any other sacred text before they give evidence to the court. However, there was a period when witnesses did have to swear by the holy book of their religion as it was thought that this would make them speak the truth. The Mughal era saw this practice transform into a system as the Hindus swore on the holy waters of the Ganga or the Bhagavad Gita and the Muslims swore by the Holy Quran. The British did not disturb this system during colonial rule but ended it in 1840, replacing it with a uniform ritual where people simply took an oath in the name of God in the courtroom. A law was enacted to end this system and put into motion in the high courts in 1863. The Indian Oaths Act of 1873 cemented this law. However, some courts like the Bombay High Court allowed non-Hindus and non-Muslims to take an oath by their religious books till 1957. A Christian had to swear by the New Testament, a Jew by the Hebrew Testament and a Parsi by the open Zend-Avesta. Only Hindus and Muslims took their oaths in the presence of the Almighty God. This practice also ended in 1969 as a law was passed to introduce a uniform system of oath-taking all over India. This holds good to date when witnesses swear by a universal God. This is how it goes: 'I do swear in the name of God/solemnly affirm that what I shall state shall be the truth, the whole truth and nothing but the truth.'

Children below twelve did not need to take an oath in court. However, some of the old Bollywood movies with courtroom scenes were fixated on witnesses taking an oath by swearing on the Bhagavad Gita. The done-to-death cliché went 'I keep my hand on the Gita and say that whatever I speak shall be the truth and nothing but the truth.'

Thankfully, even Bollywood has realized that the Constitution is the only holy book of the Indian courts. Amen to that!